Daily Telegraph

HOME OWNERSHIP A-Z

D1799429

ARTHUR BOWERS

Revised by
BRUCE KINLOCH

COLLINS
LONDON & GLASGOW

William Collins Sons & Co Ltd
London & Glasgow

First published 1977
Revised edition 1981

©*Daily Telegraph* 1977, 1981
ISBN 0 00 434186 4

Printed in Great Britain

CONTENTS

INTRODUCTION

In this book I have attempted to set out in simple form the various aspects of buying and selling a house. The idea is to take the reader easily through the many facets involved, but the book leaves off where it would be advisable for a specialist in his subject to be consulted or brought in.

As has been repeatedly pointed out, the acquisition of a house is the biggest single purchase anyone is likely to make in his or her life. It therefore follows they should be sure that what they are buying is the best they can find for what they can afford. Perhaps this book will at least help them avoid the worst pitfalls, and at best will provide some acceptable information which will be of assistance in making a choice.

Behind the whole approach is the intention to help and to warn where this is needed, the layman (or woman) who after all, is the most important person in the picture. Without his or her decision and ability to buy there would be no house market. Even so it is essential that they go the correct way about things getting both maximum value for their money and maximum satisfaction in their transactions. I have therefore attempted to clarify points which may arise or perplex and to bring forward odd pieces of information which may have been overlooked. While I have tried to cover all aspects, in as wide and general a manner as possible, the book must be regarded as a guide and not as a bible!

ARTHUR BOWERS

1981 EDITION

The number of home owners increases each year, and the dream of owning one's own home is as strong as ever among those who for one reason or another have not yet taken the plunge. Some idea of the strength of the urge to own a home can be seen from the rush by tenants of local authorities to buy now that they are free to do so.

Despite the ravages of inflation over the past decade, young people are still managing somehow to scrape together a deposit to get on the first rung of the home-ownership ladder. Alas, my colleague and friend Arthur Bowers died last year, but his book, which has helped many buyers and owners through the jungle of buying and selling houses, remains as a fitting memorial to him.

BRUCE KINLOCH

1

WHY BUY?

In these troublous times when costs of everything are going up and real values continue to fall, there is one solid investment for ordinary people – a home of their own. Houses which were built a century and more ago and which have been well looked after, restored and modernized where necessary, are worth today prices which would startle their original owners. That has not happened by chance. As the population has increased, so demand for accommodation has gone up and, with land being scarce and expensive, houses built on it have taken on an enhanced value as the years have passed.

There are very few things in this life for which a person can expect to receive more than he paid, antiques apart. A house will keep pace with inflation and most buyers who stretch themselves to become owners look back after a short while at their luck. Money invested in a house is money well spent; whatever the state of the economy it retains its value and it is an incalculable asset when the time comes to retire. It has often been said indeed, that only those owning a house can really afford to retire. Where rented property is occupied, increases can be so crippling as to force those in it out of it! With the capital bound up in a house, an owner has a choice; he may stay in it if it suits his needs and his pocket; he may sell it for something he considers more manageable under the circumstances; he may let off part of it should he so desire and at the same time provide himself with additional income, or he may dispose of it and use the money for any other purpose he likes, possibly a round-the-world trip to see his grandchildren (or to escape from them if they are too close!).

Many of those without houses tend to think those with them are lucky, but truth to tell, most have made considerable sacrifices to obtain them. More people are likely to have almost no option but to purchase in the future as there is little in the way of tenanted property available except through the various local authorities whose housing lists are already bloated. In any case, not everyone wishing to be a tenant relishes the idea of becoming a council tenant particularly as council estates have become vast concrete deserts spiked here and there with towering, impersonal blocks.

Once bought, a house is a transferable asset, usually one which appreciates in value as time goes on. That being so, home-owners are always able to change relatively easily when suitable opportunities present themselves.

About 10 per cent of the population in the British Isles move each year. Most young couples these days consider buying a home of their own simply because the alternatives usually range between crushing in with their in-laws, never a happy compromise, or being put on a waiting list for a council house, an unrewarding experience for most.

Private landlords who used to supply rented accommodation have gradually withdrawn from the market because rent controls and restrictions have made it uneconomic for them to continue in the role. It is too early to say whether the Government's short leasehold provisions will bring the private landlord back.

In practical terms it has become easier for a home-owner to change his job and his address than a tenant of a council house. The latter is unlikely to be provided with local authority accommodation should he be required to move and often the net result is that he stays put, even at the cost of losing his employment.

BUY WHAT?

House prices and values around Britain

Most people want their money to go as far as possible, with the general implication in mind that it goes farther the further a property is from main centres of population. There are broad exceptions, one being that in a number of areas where there is a demand for country houses today which was not in existence a few years ago, scarcity has enhanced values to the point where that type of property varies little in price.

While central London prices set the pace, levels are upset when special considerations, even if they are seen to be largely temporary, arise. Few for example, would have thought that a decade or so ago, a fairly modest home in Aberdeen would rank with those in the best parts of suburban London or that £100,000 would be paid for homes in the best areas convenient for those concerned with winning North Sea oil and gas. The spin-off of the new oil wealth has transformed property values on the north-east coast of Scotland and inland for some miles, and in Inverness prices for three-bedroom semi-detached homes are on a par with those in the South East of England, traditionally the top-value area. Oil and gas prospecting off the coasts of Dorset, Devon and Cornwall may also prove to be the factor which will lift levels in those counties in due course. Much however depends upon the degree of success or otherwise of the operations. Other districts in which new or expanded industry has given an impetus hitherto lacking, also are reflecting the situation in higher-than-expected prices. That is especially true of the better-quality individually-styled house which was not built to any great extent in the past. That is the position in, among other places, the Teeside

8

conurbation and in parts of the north-eastern arc in Northumberland and, specifically, Newcastle upon Tyne. Many moving from south to north are surprised that the prices they are being asked to meet are much higher than anticipated but of course, there are still many pockets where levels are distinctly depressed.

It is pertinent to illustrate the position with prices reigning during 1979 when the market had been active for some time after the slump of 1974/5 and when rises akin to those of 1972/3 had been seen. Taking central London as a base, little was offered to those unable to produce more than £15,000 though in the East London boroughs between £10,000 and £15,000 would certainly buy a small two-bedroom old terrace house, possibly not very well nor extensively modernized but capable of providing a home of sorts. Across the Metropolis a short lease on a Chelsea cottage might have been available for between £15,000 and £20,000, subject to a rent for the lease of around £500 a year. It was also possible to find a two-bedroom small flat for about £20,000, possibly in the district around Baker Street or in parts of Hampstead where a flat in a conversion from an existing building was £15,000 or so.

In the outer suburbs, where prices varied enormously according to a number of circumstances, not least the proximity or otherwise of the Underground or other station serving the capital, the £15,000 to £20,000 bracket embraced two-bedroom terrace homes to three-bedroom semi-detacheds. Under £15,000 invariably tied a buyer to a pre-1919 two-bedroom terrace house and these could be picked up in varying degrees of condition and situation.

Outside London's influence Lincolnshire, parts of Lancashire and Yorkshire and Derbyshire proved that there were still cheap buys, some for as low as £5,000 or £7,000. The £10,000 bought a four-bedroom semi-detached or terrace house in areas of Cumbria and Northumberland and Durham, even in the less popular residential districts of Newcastle upon Tyne and Sunderland, and certainly including the New Towns in the North East. In fact it was possible to pick up some four-bedroom homes for £10,000 or so in several Yorkshire and Lancashire districts. At Wakefield, one of the low-price towns in the country, older four-bedroom terrace styles were as a rule not more than £11,000, or even £10,500 in Rochdale, Lancs, and in some parts of South Liverpool. Contrastingly, on Wirral peninsula, a favourite residential area for Merseyside, a four-bedroom semi-detached was seldom less than £20,000 and usually much more, depending upon situation and condition.

One of the most straightforward guides to relative prices is the familiar two-bedroom bungalow which, outside the traditional retirement stretches of the South Coast, Kent coast, West Country and Devon and Cornwall, has a scarcity value which tends to harden the prices achieved for it. In Worthing or Eastbourne, governed to a large extent by the retirement market, the range was £14,000 to £20,000, with three-bedroom bungalows costing between £18,000 and £19,000. At Seaford, Sussex, similar homes rated £14,000 to £19,000 for two-bedroom versions, from £16,000 to £24,000 for three-bedrooms. At Brighton, an average two-bedroom bungalow at about £15,000 bore little relation to the more specialist types on selected sites for which double was paid and bungalows which in Torquay averaged about £17,000 could go up to £30,000 for those on special plots and having individual refinements. Distance not only lends enchantment to the view, but to the price, as revealed in Penzance on the tip of Britain where bungalows were found from £12,000 with three-bedroom types for £15,000 upwards. The prices at St Ives were even lower and at Newquay and Falmouth slightly higher. Some of the least expensive close to London were on the Isle of Sheppey. They were from £12,000 and at £15,000 a buyer was able to purchase an older-style three-bedroom home while similar prices were paid in some of the Medway towns. Homes in Rochester were certainly cases in point and there were cheaper buys in places like Dartford, Kent. Postwar pressure for the bungalow on the Isle of Thanet had tended to maintain levels pretty steady at Ramsgate, Margate and Broadstairs though the three towns provide slight variations even within a few miles. Being nearer London, properties in Whitstable and Herne Bay recorded prices above those on Thanet.

Where industry and commerce have been injected, demand has increased and this is reflected in the fact that a reasonable two-bedroom bungalow in Folkestone was around £15,000 and three-bedroom versions averaged £25,000.

In many London suburbs the bungalow is an elusive type of home and in the inner parts of the north and east is almost non-existent. Farther out, say at Chingford or Woodford Green, Essex, there were a few two-bedroom styles starting at £15,000 and these compared with those in Hampton at £18,000 and £20,000 at Kingston-upon-Thames. The latter figure was average too, in most Surrey dormitory towns. Armed with £28,000 to £35,000 (or even £25,000) a 1979 buyer looking outside London found he had a wide choice often including houses with five or more bedrooms and up to an acre of garden. The bracket covered small working farms in Cumbria and parts of Derbyshire, family houses in north and mid Cornwall, and smallholdings in a number of other places. These prices usually indicated that the house might need some attention as was usually the case where former farmhouses, divorced from their land, were offered as country homes with an acre or two. As well as farmhouses made redundant by amalgamations, the year saw a number of former parsonage houses being disgorged by diocesan authorities as parishes were joined and one clergyman instead of two or three took over duty. These properties too invariably required moneys spending on them to bring them up to modern standards but they did produce homes having from one to five acres for those interested in acquiring land.

What 1979 revealed too, was that there remained whole areas where it was difficult to spend £25,000 or £30,000 apart from one or two country houses which would command that and possibly more, due to the fact that they had additional land with them. It is a matter of history that because of the general pattern of industry in former days areas where homes are least costly in the lower price ranges also have the fewest properties in the higher-value categories. That is a relic of the times when there was the boss, who lived in the 'big house' and the rest, who lived in terrace rows in the village.

In the £30,000 to £35,000 group, in London it was found that a three-bedroom unimposing terrace house in Kensington would cost within that bracket, though some of these homes reached £50,000 and more. There were in Notting Hill Gate the odd four-bedroom styles though the bracket excluded generally even three-bedroom terrace properties in St John's Wood. At the same time, West Hampstead and Wembley could both produce up to five bedrooms in older styles for £27,000 to £35,000, and there were flats and maisonettes from West Brompton to Chelsea, Blackheath to Putney and Ealing, Hampstead or Richmond, Surrey.

In Richmond, Yorkshire, on the other hand, a buyer would have his pick of the market apart from a few of the most distinguished houses there which sold for more than £35,000, while across country at Carlisle the range for anything rarely exceeded £30,000. Nor did it at Hexham, Northumberland or on the Northumbrian coast at Whitley Bay or Tynemouth. Much of the North East and North West has limited categories with only certain parts of certain towns producing properties which break into the higher-value ranges. For instance, it was possible to spend £20,000 to £25,000 relatively easily in the best districts of Harrogate, the Yorkshire spa which has emerged as a dormitory for Leeds. At the same time it was difficult to find houses of the calibre which commanded those prices in York, which is more self-contained and is without the pressures for living space from those whose interests are centred on a major city. Some of the Yorkshire coastal towns, Scarborough among them, and its little brother, Filey, also produce better houses than those of their inland neighbours like Tadcaster, where, as a general rule there were few sales at more than £30,000. Usually that was for one of the more spectacular houses or bungalows of which there were few available. While there is a large retirement population at St Annes, in the Blackpool orbit, the same observation applies and there are very sound four-bedroom homes which changed hands in 1979 for £15,000 to £28,000, including bungalows of quite large proportions. Nearby at Fleetwood, prices were seen to be easier while at Southport, £22,000 to £27,000 went a long way. Such a sum was certainly sufficient to acquire a detached five- or six-bedroom house as it was in Buxton, Derbyshire's inland spa, in Nottingham and in much of Wales.

It may easily be deduced therefore that most fortunate from a price point of view are home-owners who can take their skills or businesses anywhere in the country and are not obliged, like the majority, to find a house or flat near their office, factory or shop. As a guide, the traditional estate-style three-bedroom semi-detached house can be bought in parts of the north of England and in Northern Ireland, as well as on the Borders of Scotland, and certainly on most of the Western Isles, for half or less of its cost in the residential suburbs of London or Birmingham.

That however, is not the true total story. In industrial areas where there have been fewer other types of homes built over the years price gaps narrow, although in general terms homes are still less expensive in places where semis are cheapest.

In every district there are pockets of higher-value housing which may bear little relation to prices in the rest of the area. There are, inevitably, local conditions and associations which have produced that state of affairs and anyone contemplating a new and unknown part should spend some time finding out about them.

Except in those traditional retirement regions, bungalows may be said to be relatively expensive everywhere while in some places they are so scarce as to be non-existent in general terms. Where there have been built what are known as 'one-off' bungalows, that is a home built specially for someone or to an individual design, and on a site of its own, the price can literally be anything within reason and, sometimes, outside reason! It all depends upon the demand for it and simply, how much someone is willing to pay for it.

The housing market

Prices of course, are liable to change and it is wise to follow their reactions to certain circumstances. In common with every other commodity, property reacts to boom and slump conditions and to everything in between. As a result, at times when money is scarce and expensive to obtain, prices are likely to be more static than when funds are more freely available. Sellers tend to keep out of the market when they can expect less for their houses than they would like, and, of course, re-enter it when they think circumstances are more favourable.

Even so, there are few periods when real scarcity prevents an assiduous buyer from finding what he wants. The point is, can he afford it? While in general terms a person is well-advised to pay out as much as he possibly can for a home, it is necessary to cut one's housecoat according to one's cloth. What does occur at various times in the market is that there are more homes available in certain price brackets at certain periods and market conditions regulate how these are spread. A temptation therefore at those times is to take on a property which is either less than can be afforded, or more than can be managed.

12

It is always wise to discuss requirements with an agent, really discuss, not just accept a list of houses available. Though he is pledged to do the best he can for his client, that basically means selling the latter's house for him. It is a waste of everyone's time and effort to have long discussions on houses which are entirely unsuitable, more so if the process also involves viewing them. Though agents are bound to put all offers made for houses to their clients, the sellers, they do have a great deal of influence with them and the highest offer does not always necessarily result in a satisfactory sale. Very often a smaller offer which is not only genuine but also available immediately provides a better deal for the seller as well as for the person making it. Of major concern must always be the condition of a property. Those which are in dilapidated state may be cheaper but by the time money is expended on them to make them habitable by today's standards they may be anything but cheap. Others well-kept, in good decorative order and qualifying for peak prices in their category may be a far better buy, especially as a building society will advance a much bigger loan on them. Size, too, is all important. When economics dictate that belts must be tightened, large and expensive-to-run houses can be picked up relatively inexpensively while smaller houses which are more easily maintained and serviced can look expensive by comparison. Though the price paid for a home is a once-for-all outlay, the cost of running it goes on increasing year by year as charges for rates, electricity, gas and water go up.

The house market is seasonal in many respects. Spring obviously, is an active period, when properties are looking at their best, and winter is slackest, for the obvious opposite reason. There are exceptions proving the rule; sometimes there are bursts of unaccountable activity in mid summer or around Christmas and New Year. This is probably due to the fact that applications for loans which had been made earlier suddenly transpired and with the offer of finance buyers immediately went ahead, whatever the season.

The aim should be to buy and sell 'in the same market' that is, with as little time between the transactions as possible. In that way, higher prices for selling match higher prices for purchasing and, of course, the converse is also true.

There are periods when sellers are at a disadvantage. For example, during 1975 the market was sluggish; there were few buyers around and those who were interested in acquiring a house not only had a wide choice, but because of this, prices became depressed. Lack of competition meant that sellers who sold first were those who dropped their asking prices as low as possible. The economic recession allied with rising living costs also meant that in 1975 and 1976, people who were interested in buying homes had a limited amount of money for the purpose and not much leeway. They too, tended to keep prices down by searching the market for properties reckoned to be pitched low.

For a seller this meant that, if he had to sell, possibly because his job had changed and he was required to move, he did so quickly only if his offer was the best, that is, the cheapest, of all those around him. Because of that situation he was limited too in the price he was able to pay in the new area to which he had gone. The effect was cumulative and so prices remained fairly static.

After a period in 1974/5 when the market stabilized and sellers found that the prices which had been obtained in the boom years of 1972/3 were no longer the norm, there was a fresh rise in the market, largely as a result of continuing inflation and escalation in earnings. An idea of what had happened by 1979 can be gained from the fact that in London's main residential districts like Kensington, Knightsbridge and Chelsea, homes which had reached a peak of £60,000 in 1972/3 were changing hands for £75,000. In the higher priced houses in these areas, which usually contradict the prevailing condition of an excess of demand for houses over supply, there was an even larger increase as Arab buyers entered the market and houses of £100,000 to £500,000 doubled in price.

A striking feature of the market in recent years has been this appearance of Middle East purchasers. Mainly from the oil states and benefitting from the 1973 massive increase in oil prices, they took to London as a stable financial centre in preference to war-torn Beirut and were ready and willing to meet high prices. Even though the amounts involved were often substantial, the prices at which these buyers obtained houses and flats as well as landed estates close to London, could be considered bargains compared with their earlier values. Arab sheikhs, Turkish and Persian businessmen have been prominent purchasers, along with Europeans, Americans and Canadians who have interests in this country.

The different types of homes

Builders naturally, are less concerned with the spectacular and concentrate their activities providing what they feel is best for the majority. Throughout the country therefore the most prolific house is the three-bedroom semi-detached type. Every town and village has at least a few and most of the larger cities have thousands. They are chosen by both private developers and local authorities as being the ideal style for the majority of families, being small enough for a couple to acquire either by purchase or to rent, satisfactory for bringing up a family, at any rate in the early years of children's lives, and not too unmanageable for persons who prefer to stay in them when they are elderly. The alternatives, the two-bedroom semi and the four- and five-bedroom styles obviously do not easily match up, the former tending to be too cramped for family living and the latter too large for a couple whose family has grown up and left. Though broadly, the three-bedroom semi

14

is basically the same, there are several different sizes and modifications which attract various buyers in various ways.

It has been discovered, for example, that semi-detached styles in certain areas, particularly in the northern half of the country, sell best and are most popular when they have bay windows. One postwar developer found this to his cost when he created an estate of semis with flat fronts and wondered why they did not sell, while his competitors whose houses were given bays could not build them fast enough to meet the demand! Some semis are built with bay windows at both ground and first floor level at the front; others have bays at the back as well. There are refinements in many such as French doors from the dining or drawing room, specially constructed halls to take a pram, open-plans which provide a large circulating area incorporating the whole of a ground floor excluding the kitchen, and so on.

While the Victorians did build semi-detached houses, the greatest drive was during the late 1920s and throughout the 1930s, and, again, after the 1939–45 war when building really recommenced in the 1950s. Postwar shortages were felt for many years and houses were only built under licence for a decade, but during the 1960s and early 1970s hundreds of estates of semis went up, many unrelieved by any attempt to vary the external appearance and possibly only differing inside by the colour of the bathroom suites! Many buyers began to foresake the semi because of this and sought homes, even semis, which were 'not on an estate'. Financial considerations however, often determined that they had little choice but to purchase a semi on an estate whether they liked it or not! What many of them meant of course, was that estates, being new, looked stark and dreary. Recent emphasis, both voluntarily and officially enforced, on retaining trees, has considerably helped to offset the sameness which otherwise can become overbearing.

Inflation has hit the semi, like everything else. As inflation has increased, space in the semi has decreased; as prices have gone up buyers have got less for their money. That fact has turned many would-be owners of a semi to look to those built before 1939 and it is acknowledged that the dozen years before the outbreak of the last war were vintage years for that style of building. A sound prewar semi is invariably better value for money than any built in recent times as it is likely to contain 1,000 or more square feet compared with some of those constructed in the past few years which have been as little as 630 square feet, albeit built to designs which to be fair, belie the paucity of space. As costs went up steadily in 1976 the concern of builders was apparent; their costs were well ahead of prices for which their wares would sell. It was estimated that on average, a semi was taking £2,000 more to build than buyers were willing to pay, with the net result that house-building slowed down considerably.

Statistics prove that most buyers would prefer a new house, but there is something to be said too, in favour of acquiring one already

15

'run in' and the range of these is extensive. At the same time, it is obvious that anyone seeking something 'different' is invariably faced with purchasing secondhand. Much time and trouble has been taken to bring into use the vast numbers of late-Victorian and Edwardian terrace houses to be seen in most towns and cities. To modernize such properties often means, if they are small, that a bedroom is sacrificed to provide a bathroom, though in some cases where the space exists, it has been possible to build on to form a kitchen at ground level with bathroom above to preserve a third bedroom. A drawback to the majority of the smallest pre-1919 terrace houses is that they are confined to two bedrooms and the staircases are narrow and steep. They do however, offer an opportunity to newly-weds to get a foot on the buying 'ladder', the next step invariably being to a semi. Fortunately, the older terrace houses do vary in size and, to a lesser extent in style. There are those with their bay windows and with attic accommodation as well as cellars, some of the best provide spacious rooms ideal for families, others unfortunately will never be anything more than they are; just very old, tired, worn-out buildings better replaced with something new.

Attempts made to create inexpensive alternatives include schemes for flats and maisonettes, but it has taken some time for these to be accepted. As alternatives to bungalows in many areas traditionally favoured by those nearing or having reached retirement age, the problem persists. In some cases, these alternatives are not yet fully integrated and there are several instances where public opinion is firmly against that type of accommodation.

Land shortages, combined with its high cost in recent years, prompted changes so that the bungalow, which uses up more space laterally, found itself continually in a state of siege from both planners and builders. Along with the general attitude towards bungalows planners began a process to encourage employment in traditional retirement areas, particularly in resort towns, to correct imbalances in population caused by young people having to move away to find jobs. This caused new responsibilities for housing with some slant towards providing family homes as distinct from retirement bungalows, as well as flats and maisonettes suitable for both young and old. It is because of that that bungalows have assumed a scarcity value which has enhanced their prices. Broadly it may be estimated that a two-bedroom bungalow costs about the same as a three-bedroom house while a flat or maisonette is £1,000 to £2,000 below the latter.

Contrary as ever, the public has reacted in unpredictable fashion. Many young couples have competed with the elderly for bungalows on the grounds that they are more easily maintained and less costly to paint because they do not require ladders to be raised. At the same time many owners of large family houses with substantial gardens have taken on a flat because it is easy to run, generally with any common ground being taken care of on a communal basis. The smaller and less luxurious flats and maisonettes have however, filled a necessary gap for those with more limited means. Flats and maisonettes are most popular with all ages where they are close to town centres, convenient for shops and services and because they can be locked up with a fair knowledge that they will not easily be broken into if their owners are absent over lengthy periods.

With large houses becoming too expensive for many to continue to run and where seaside hotels have become obsolescent due to the changes in patterns of holidays they are being replaced with varying-size blocks. Such flats provide sea views for owners who otherwise would not have been able to afford a waterfront house. These days it is usual for flats and maisonettes to have central heating and domestic hot water.

Those bent on a bungalow must be prepared to be farther from town centres, particularly if they wish to buy new. To be closer invariably means purchasing secondhand.

Loans are available for flats and maisonettes in the same way as for other properties, but not every building society or insurance company will consider them. It is thus necessary to shop around for one which will lend on flats. Normally such societies insist that flats are leasehold so that there is control over the building by the freeholder.

Under all the circumstances, the traditional bungaloid areas are being superseded by others, generally based on inland villages where country scenery replaces sight and sound of the sea. Many villages, for example those in the Yorkshire Dales which are easily accessible from the more densely-packed West Riding industrial conurbations are increasingly catering for the bungalow-seeker. In such spots, flats and maisonettes will not be given much countenance. Land is not so scarce in these villages and hamlets, though attention is paid to building styles and materials which are expected to blend in with the natural surroundings. Sometimes the bungalow schemes are spiced with small blocks of maisonettes but only where they can be successfully integrated visually; in fact to look as if they are anything but flats! There is a limited demand in most places, even in the smallest hamlet, for this type of flatted accommodation as it suits the elderly who find stairs a problem. They of course specify ground floor accommodation anyway! Prices are governed as much by where these homes are as by what they are. Where pressures on land have been few because it is at some distance from main towns, then prices have tended to be easier, though this must be qualified to take into account villages which have built up a special reputation. Prizes for being the best-kept or most painted are likely to rub off on property prices. Popularity must be paid for if such notoriety is to be shared in! That is a fact reflected in London prices too as anyone armed with the proceeds from a sale, say in Chelsea, can testify to.

While London sets the pace for the rest of the country its least expensive districts are less only by comparison with what the same article will cost elsewhere. Nearly everywhere houses in the western arc are more expensive than those in the east; north, in general is cheaper than south, but there are pockets in all areas which are highly-priced and keenly sought. As far as London is concerned, the inner suburbs of the east and north are comparatively inexpensive with exceptions where older period houses have been given face lifts and where, because of the attempts by various well-known people to raise the standard of a street or district, it has become fashionable to live. Several of the squares in Islington provide examples of this situation. Some of the least expensive buys are found in parts of Cumbria, Cornwall, Derbyshire, Durham, North Yorkshire and Northumbria, the Border country, Wales and in Scotland away from the influence of North Sea oil and of the industrialized major towns including Glasgow and Edinburgh. Careful probing in those regions will disclose how much more a purchaser is offered for the £30,000 to £35,000 or less demanded for properties in the Home Counties.

Overall there appears to be an increase in the numbers of those willing to take over and improve properties in hitherto unpopular, decayed or unfashionable districts. Much has to do with keeping expenses to a minimum so that home-owning is taking on trends which were unknown in earlier days when there was a bigger gap between the haves, the hope-to-haves and the have-nots. A legacy is seen in many of our towns where large Victorian unwieldy properties, some with up to 20 rooms, recall the 19th-century families, well-heeled, with hordes of children and well-served from below by an army of domestic servants. Numbers of these 'Upstairs, Downstairs' homes which had been vacated, have been acquired for splitting up in various ways; horizontally and vertically as well as into flats and maisonettes. Depending upon how these large houses have been maintained so the amount of work required to be done on them is regulated, but anyone purchasing such a building for transforming into several self-contained homes can find it reasonably profitable if the job is carried out properly. Obviously, an owner will necessarily have to be able to call on considerably more finance than the initial cost of the property, which, in relation to its size, could be fairly cheap.

It is common in these times for several families to band together to buy and convert houses and financial institutions can be sympathetic if plans presented to them appear to be viable propositions. Planning consents are required and it is likely that there could be grants to assist with the provision of basic amenities. It would be a wise precaution to talk over proposals with the local authority's planning officials before making a decision to purchase. An advantage from an owner's point of view is that he is able generally, to acquire for himself in the process of providing others with a home also, for a relatively small

18

figure against the accommodation he gets. Normally too, such large older houses occupy generous sites and the new home-owners invariably find themselves with a garden sufficiently large to enable them all to have a considerable slice. Grounds usually contain mature trees which in turn afford the residents as much privacy as they would be ever likely to want.

At the same time, other old town houses, many in multiple occupation and in streets which were considered to be beyond the pale for ordinary living, have been restored as individual family homes and the practice of renovation has caught and continues to catch on.

At the other end of the scale are cottages, coming in all shapes and sizes, costing all manner of prices. Some of the least expensive areas for them are Lincolnshire, parts of Wales and East Anglia, and the less salubrious areas of Yorkshire and Lancashire. Many of the former pit villages are now spruced up since the collieries have closed and houses once accommodating miners and their families are often available though at figures much higher than would previously have been the case. Most expensive cottages are closest to the large cities but in rural situations. The Home Counties, the West Country, Herefordshire and Worcestershire are happy hunting grounds and in some of these districts homes doubtless starting out as modest enough cottages have been expanded and transformed into four- and five-bedroom houses retaining only the cottage tag in their names.

It is increasingly difficult to find cottages and other buildings suitable for complete renovation as most have been improved and modernized to some degree at least. Generally they get on to the market where they have been occupied by long-standing tenants who either move away or die. Instead of reletting them the owners prefer to sell them off. It is a sensible move however for a prospective purchaser of a cottage or house to look out for one on which his individual stamp would be imprinted with additions made to his liking. Alternatively, such individuality could well involve demolition of unwanted or dilapidated unattractive extensions.

Among those prominent in the cottage market are couples seeking a retirement home. Frequently they find it convenient to buy before they actually require the property and may wish to let it meantime. Should such a decision be made, care must be taken to have drawn up an agreement with potential tenants which ensures that a cottage is vacated when the owners require it for their own occupation. The various Rent Acts have given tenants added security so that a legally-drawn-up document is vital. Very often it is a good deal safer to offer the accommodation to a foreign tenant, or, if possible to a foreign government for use of their servants. In any event, it is essential that expert legal advice is obtained and followed in the case of such agreements. Unless it is (and indeed very possibly because it is) vacant possession of a cottage which has been let will involve an owner going to court to prove greater need of the property. There is no guarantee that the court's sympathy will be with him in his plea for possession of the cottage and in fact even if his application for possession is not refused it may be made subject to considerable delay. There is also nothing to stop a tenant continually applying for an extension of occupation, thus prolonging his use of the accommodation.

Among the attractions of those cottages which are rurally-sited on individual plots, are the generous gardens which invariably go with them. Contrastingly in modern housing generally on estates, much has been sacrificed in the way of gardens. Postage-stamp plots where homes are constructed at up to 16 and 20 to the acre, do not leave much ground for individual cultivation or enjoyment and whether it is medically acknowledged or not, lack of privacy, as a result, has had much to do with the dissatisfaction expressed in many unsocial ways.

It took some time for planners to realize that tower blocks of flats were not the ideal answer to the housing problem, nor do they, because of the ratio of building to site area, save very much more, if any, land compared with laterally-built terraces or groups of dwellings. Frustration is revealed in many forms, not least by the continual efforts of the occupants of tower blocks to encourage window boxes to thrive up on the 20th floor. Young mothers have discovered that there are many more frustrations associated with high living. It is beyond a joke, when, having descended from the 16th floor (after a prolonged wait for the only lift which appears to be untouched by vandals), little Johnny decides he must have the needs of nature attended to, and quickly! At the opposite end of the age scale, elderly couples feel and are, isolated on the upper floors, where it is difficult to meet friends or make acquaintances.

There is a case for flats, but rarely of more than five storeys and preferably of only three. Flats have eased the lot of many old and infirm people, relieving them of the necessity of looking after, or of having looked after, gardens which have become too much of a strain upon them. Nevertheless, there is a solid backing for gardens from the younger elements in the population, and houses with what is vaguely described as 'a bit of land' are among the most favoured purchases.

To some extent gardens go in and out of fashion, but at the same time they do end many frustrations, providing children with a play space and parents with an interest which costs little and is most rewarding both in terms of money and benefits to health. No one quite knows where a 'garden' ends and 'a bit of land' starts, but those who have either or both are aware of their value. When motoring is relatively inexpensive and parents use the weekends to take their children away into the country, gardens can be a worry and a drudge. At times when economies must be practised, gardens replace the weekend jaunts and the vegetables which can be grown not only save the distaff side money but taste better too.

Thus do gardens play their part and in recent years increasing numbers have been seeking homes having more than the restricted plot usual on postwar developments. Attractions for the house with land as well as a garden are based on the requirement of having somewhere for the children's ponies and donkeys to run. The paddock, particularly with waterside grazing, is keenly sought. Sometimes, where more land has to be acquired than is needed by the family's pursuits, a neighbouring farmer requires little persuasion to take it over on a rented basis to cultivate or run his cattle.

While it is true to say that the majority of people like to see a well-kept and tilled garden, by no means everyone wants the work of attending to it, either himself or by hiring labour, which is expensive these days. It is, therefore, vitally necessary to consider, when thinking of buying a house, just how much the garden or grounds impinges on the decision. There is little point in taking over a home having a huge garden if all that will happen is that it will be neglected and become an eyesore. Nothing looks, or is, worse than an overgrown and untended plot.

On the other hand there are ways of making a garden 'look' after itself to some degree at least. Much can be planted with quick-growing shrubs and plants which spread and cover weeds, with lawns which need mainly only cutting if an owner is not too particular. Cutting today can be a pleasant occupation if a mower incorporating a seat is acquired for the purpose! Coloured paving is also a clever way of maintaining space while cutting down maintenance to a minimum and, if funds run to it, a good chunk of a large garden can be successfully devoured by the excavation of a swimming pool!

Low-cost housing

Because it has never been easy for the first-time purchaser to rake together the necessary funds to buy, attempts have been made over the years by builders to meet his pocket. Low-cost housing has as a result, become a popular target at which to aim but land prices in recent years dictated largely what style of home could be produced. In most of the central areas of our cities, blocks of flats have superseded former town houses and on estates terrace types have been built instead of semi-detached and detached. Only in certain areas has it been possible to erect bungalows falling into low-cost categories and even these have on occasion been in terraces.

While most builders and developers favour the traditional estate-style three-bedroom semi-detached house, a tried and trusted product over many years, they have found that most first-time buyers have not been able to stretch to their prices. Accordingly they have trimmed their programmes to include small flats and two-bedroom terrace styles. It has been found that it was also desirable, from a pure cost basis, to build on out-of-town sites where land could usually be acquired more heaply than closer to built-up areas. There are cases where developers and builders have provided 'starter homes' which allow for the basic structure to be extended at a later date and others who have constructed the essentials in a 'shell' leaving the buyers to complete the internal finishes. There have also been economies made in the facilities for parking and in the standards of estate roads.

Extendable houses in general have not caught on very quickly though apparently the acceptance or otherwise of this principle has depended upon the initial reaction. Homes which 'grow' according to the increasing demands on space of the family are however, carving out a niche for themselves. A key factor in builders' continual exploration of the possibilities of the extendable house has been the desire that further accommodation could be added without too much effort and expense. If the experience of the firm of C. S. Wiggins & Son, on an Essex site, can be taken as a barometer, the aim has been to keep the cost below price levels which broadly apply to the area, while at the same time providing all the necessary 'engineering' for future expansion. A garage and standard garden are included and the roof already contains the necessary windows for when the top floor is pressed into service. The basic structure is suited for the single person, elderly couple or newly-marrieds. The roofspace is used for the extra rooms which will be required when family needs so dictate. The Wiggins approach obviates the need for more foundations and cavity walls which exterior extensions necessitate. All that is required is the installation of stairs and the finished partitioning in the roofspace to provide one, two or three bedrooms.

As sold the basic house contains kitchen, bathroom, hall and living room which doubles as a bedroom, plus a garage capable of taking two small cars or, if preferred to serve as a workshop or play area. Power and lighting circuits are arranged so that additional points can be installed. Estimates indicate that up to £4,000 or £5,000 can be saved by this type of expansion compared with an external extension at the back or side of an existing property for a one-room addition. Surveys undertaken into the question of starter homes have revealed that it is low-cost homes rather than small homes which are most acceptable and most required. On the other hand, many young couples out at work all day found it an advantage to have less space to look after. In some parts of the country, the Greaves Organization has undertaken both starter homes and what are described as Heritage homes. The latter are attractive for older people who have sold the family house. Half the proceeds of the sale are invested in a Heritage home, smaller, cheaper and easier to maintain and run, and the remainder in an annuity to provide additional income. The homes are sold on a leasehold basis to ensure proper maintenance of common areas and facilities which include landscaped gardens and an emergency call system. A condition of the lease is that resales are only to people aged 45 or more. These properties are finished to higher standards than the starter homes which are kept at the least expensive levels possible. Like Greaves, Shepherds build for these markets while William Whittingham found that one-bedroom flats were popular.

How to choose a home

Not every type of property is available where it is desired in every district. Everyone knows where he would like to be as well as what he would like to have. Unfortunately for most the ultimate must wait and sometimes it is never achieved. The majority discover a satisfactory compromise and in time are so comfortably placed that they are loath ever to move again. At first the decision must be taken about where a purchase is to be made. It is fairly pointless to crash about here, there and everywhere weekend in and weekend out and the key is to decide upon an area then search for a suitable place.

For most, the area is dictated by the type and place of their employment and the idea increasingly is to cut down travelling to be as close to work as is possible. That factor itself is a limiting one, but again should be matched against other considerations. A family man must obviously have cognizance of the needs of his wife and children. Thus the proximity of schools, shops, churches and other facilities comes into the reckoning. Ages of children too, are important. Teenagers have a dislike of being too far from their friends and long journeys taking them first to school, bringing them home, taking them out again in the evenings or weekends so that they can attend youth clubs or follow their sporting instincts cease to be funny after a while. It is also an expensive luxury when father or mother is chauffeur to the youngsters in the family car. It is also more expensive if, because of distance, a second or even a third car has to be maintained so that the wives are not cut off from reasonable human contact all day. There is some limit on situation caused by purse strings. In towns, the oldest houses, among them the cheapest, are closest to centres with the younger and generally more expensive properties radiating from them. Depending upon how near a town centre a buyer wishes to be so the age and invariably the price are broadly set.

On the other hand, in a number of towns, period properties close to the town centres have been modernized and restored. These, despite their ages, are bought for what they are and prices can vary enormously. A well-modernized period house in a nicely-renovated street can command a very high figure. Several have been turned into office accommodation for professional people, but this practice has largely been halted by the planning authorities which now prefer them to be lived in again.

What must never be forgotten is that situation is the main attribute for a house. A good house in a bad situation will be of lesser value than

23

a bad house in a good position. Situation, like everything else, tends to change with the times, though there are one or two secondary factors to be remembered. Some properties have declined in popularity and value because traffic has been routed through the streets on which they stand; others have been allowed to deteriorate where they have adjoined others occupied for many years by tenants and landlords who have progressively neglected them. Whole neighbourhoods have become classed as unsavoury or are unwanted because of the substantial amounts of substandard properties in them. Such local points should be carefully observed. At the same time, in many towns, streets once run-down are being brought up with council encouragement. Grants available for modernizing substandard homes are available and local authorities are ready in some cases to play their part by creating green areas and small gardens and sometimes by closing off a street or two to form a cul-de-sac. Values in such streets are rising and there are 'Little Chelseas' all over the country now!

It is true, however amazing it may seem, that very few people generally and genuinely know what they really want to buy. Much buying is done on the spur of the moment. A couple may be out for a drive when they see a house they like and decide there and then, that if it is within their ability, they will have it. Others search around not knowing really what they are looking for and hoping they will get ideas by just gazing. For the majority, financial limits set levels about what to buy, as well as where it can be bought. Again it is the compromise which can turn out to be advantageous and quite acceptable in the long run. Many a couple who bought modestly have reason to thank themselves for adopting that course in view of consistent and swingeing increases in the cost of living! At the same time, buyers should purchase a property valued as high as they can reasonably afford. Unlike almost everything else, bricks and mortar do keep pace with rises in living costs (or in other times, they fall in value at the same rate), so that a house maintains its value as an investment come what may. Should prices fall, then a seller is able to take advantage of that fact by purchasing more cheaply too. All the other things we use; cars, furniture, clothes, for example, have a much diminished secondhand value. A house bought this year usually seems relatively cheap when looked at two or three years hence, as meantime incomes have risen and in addition the cost of producing that same house has also gone up. In effect, selling it will certainly show a profit of some sort, disregarding the fact that if a couple did not have a house of their own they would be paying out rent anyway.

Given the will and the wherewithal to acquire a place of one's own, the great thing is to buy *something*. Starting to climb the ladder of buying is the vital move so that standards can be bettered as one moves up the salary scale. It is thus seen that an essential element is the first-time purchaser who has very modest means but who is prepared to take on a small house possibly even to 'do up' to some degree himself. Without the first-time purchaser on the lowest rung of the ladder, the whole buying chain can be interrupted as indeed happened in 1977 when prices put many of that category of purchaser out of the running until wages caught up again.

While the aim should be to acquire as expensively as funds allow, care to keep within proper limits is also necessary. Overreaching can have unfortunate results if, for instance, mortgage repayments become too high to maintain or unexpected increases in other commodities, particularly food, fuel for heating and lighting, and rates, stretch the hard-earned pound too far. Remember Mr Micawber: 'Annual income £20, annual expenditure £19 19s 6d, result happiness. Annual income £20, expenditure £20 0s 6d, result misery'.

Naturally, the amount which can be paid for a property does to an extent dictate what can be bought, but there is room for manoeuvre within that limit. Always remember that in most towns the oldest houses are closest to the centre with younger properties radiating from them and that too, has a bearing on price.

There are however, broad decisions to be made. For some, a flat is more convenient than a house; for others a bungalow may be preferred to either. For those who dislike gardening and cannot afford a gardener it is pointless to buy a property having a large plot. Those who do like gardening will be frustrated on a small site. Some prefer an old house to a modern one; others like to have a place which gives scope for restoration or redecoration, extension or contraction. Some wish to have a home which has historical or architectural associations, all the better to show off to friends (or enemies), others seek out the contemporary and unusual again for the same reason. There are those who wish to be close to water, or in a windmill or oast-house and so it goes on!

As a general guide it may be indicated that the least expensive homes are those built between 1880 and 1910 mainly in long terraces in industrial areas. They were constructed for workers in various factories and other undertakings, and they vary very little though there are two- and three-bedroom styles. Some have front doors opening directly on to the pavement; some have small front gardens. Nearly all have back yards or gardens and sometimes both. They are unprepossessing, visually can be made attractive when fully modernized, are cosy, easy to heat but can be rather cramped. Towards 1914 larger types were built in some areas to be followed after the end of the First World War in the 1920s by terrace properties of better proportions and certainly with better regulated internal layout.

A mainstay from the 1920s, with occasionally earlier ones of Victorian and Edwardian vintage, has been the three-bedroom semi-detached house. Most of the best were built in the 1930s along what have become residential roads as distinct from estate developments which

25

have been the rule rather than the exception since the end of the last war.

BUY HOW?

Buying with the help of a loan

As buying a property is a major step, for most people the most important deal they will ever make, it should not be undertaken lightly nor should anything be rushed. Decisions should only be made and acted upon after careful thought and as a result of advice if such is considered necessary – and it usually pays off even if it has to be paid for!

It is estimated that between 90 and 95 per cent of all homes bought are acquired with the help of a loan. Along with a loan a buyer must have some money of his own to use as a deposit and also to give him a stake in the home he is purchasing. Time is well spent shopping around, investigating the possibilities and cost of taking out a mortgage for this purpose. Most borrowers obtain their mortgages from one of the hundreds of building societies, large and small, which operate throughout the country. Their terms and conditions, though broadly the same, do vary in detail so that it is worth finding out which are most suited to individual needs. Valuable help can be given in this respect by a mortgage broker. It is wise to deal with those brokers who are members of the Corporation of Mortgage and Finance Brokers. Members may be recognized by the initials after their names; FCMB (Fellow of the Corporation, Incorporated member-firm) and ACMB (Associate of the Corporation, Incorporated member-firm). They have undertaken to abide by a strict code of conduct in business transactions.

One of the best pieces of advice anyone can be given is to start saving with a building society. In that way, it is possible to build up a sum to be used as a deposit for a home. Another, and equally important aspect of saving with a society is that when the time comes for a mortgage to be sought, preference is invariably given to 'members' of a society as savers with them are called. When mortgage funds are tight, as they are from time to time, to be a saver with a society ensures that if there is money available for a loan, the member is more likely to be considered than a casual applicant.

An alternative is to take out an insurance policy with an assurance company which is specially earmarked for buying a house at a future date. Invariably in these cases, the company will also advance the balance of the money required to purchase when the time comes, though it will insist on insurance cover to the value of the mortgage.

When it comes to house purchase, the thing to do is to start things off as early in life as possible. The sooner initial steps are taken the easier it is. As the years roll on the problem of taking out a generous mortgage increases to the point where none is available! At 25, a loan over 25 years runs out quite nicely at 50; or, should a person wish to change houses in between, the equity he has built up in his existing house and the reputation he has made with the building society helping him buy stand him in good stead for further help. Building societies, as well as God, help those who help themselves!

Thinking of buying a first house at 50 or over is something most building societies treat somewhat disdainfully unless of course, the applicant is one of its 'members', that is, an investor with them. To become an investor is simple; merely use the society of one's choice as a savings institution, putting in amounts regularly and receiving interest, tax-paid, on them. In such cases, an elderly applicant would normally be expected to use his invested capital whereas a younger person may find that his society is willing to allow him a greater percentage of the necessary money involved in his purchase, thus preserving more of his capital intact. The situation and method very much depend upon which is the more advantageous from a tax point of view. An elderly applicant in any case would have less need to maintain a large capital sum which would be better invested in bricks and mortar. Any society in which he had chosen to invest would invariably be prepared to advance him a relatively small topping-up loan to seal a bargain.

Above 50, applicants will find that their applications for mortgages are very much treated on their merits. In most cases, advances, if they are made at all, are rarely for more than 10 years. In certain instances there may be exceptions to the rule with loans of 15 years taking them through to the normal retirement age for men. Societies generally are chary about granting such extensions fearing that there may be incapacity interfering with earnings as the years creep on. Some notable exceptions are however, made in the cases of applicants who are employed by local and central government agencies. Well-placed are civil servants and others, who, at 50, can continue to look forward to steady increments in salary plus a pension which reflects and will go on reflecting the cost of living. As far as a society is concerned, the view is taken that anyone having a Civil Service position will, by the time he retires have a pension likely to match his present salary. On retirement he is also normally entitled to between a third and a quarter of his salary as a lump payment and so is in good standing to be able to pay off any mortgage he might have. Unlike his counterpart in outside employment, a Civil Service applicant would be granted a loan for 25, instead of 10 to 15 years, the idea being that when he was granted his lump sum payment he could use it to pay off all or at least some, of the money outstanding. With a fair-size pension as his entitlement anyway he would be in a position to maintain the repayments of the loan. At the point of retirement a society would be prepared to talk over any adjustments considered mutually beneficial and make them then and there. In cases other than local or national government officers and their quasi-governmental colleagues, a building society would wish to know, before committing itself in advance, what anyone had been doing all his life with his income if he still required a substantial mortgage. Unless there were very satisfactory and straightforward reasons, such an applicant would not be tagged as very credit-worthy. Whether or not a society would advance a smallish sum would depend upon what were a person's prospects so far as his or her job and pension were concerned.

It is an open secret that there are certain classifications and categories from which most societies shy away. Among these are sales managers, who may, at 45 or 50 be earning £15,000 or £16,000 a year but who could, because of the uncertainties of trade, lose their jobs at the drop of a pound. Other people in such trade-orientated employment also find it difficult to obtain loans in later life.

Summer months too, encourage many nearing retirement age to earmark country districts or seaside resorts, and in some instances a particular house as well, as suited for their more leisurely days, holidays, a second home or a pre-purchase in advance of giving up work. Building societies are not notably lavish with applicants who wish to buy such properties and in the event it is wise to consider that they must be cash purchases. In any case there are now no tax advantages as there used to be in borrowing to acquire a home other than what is designated one's main place of residence and there is Capital Gains Tax in the offing when one or both properties come to be dispensed with. Even building societies, which might be sympathetic, like least those transactions to do with second or holiday homes which owners may wish to let when they do not require them for their own occupation. That goes equally for the property at the seaside or in the country acquired in advance of retirement but which will later become the purchaser's only home.

Building societies are reluctant to be involved in properties which are tenanted, though some will accept them where special considerations exist. For example, a person buying his house through a building society who is then posted abroad for a term, will be given permission under normal circumstances to allow his property to accommodate a tenant on the understanding that the latter will evacuate the premises when they are again required by the buying owner. Income from rents in such cases easily cover the outgoings for mortgage and insurance. If however, there is any question over future possession of a property building societies really would not rather know and will certainly not wish to become involved. As every application to borrow is treated strictly on merit, a first 'no' is not necessarily the last word, and while there is virtue in shopping around a bit on the off chance, the real secret is to have taken the precaution early on in becoming an investor and thereby gaining whatever advantages there are. Non-investors, and indeed, some investors dissatisfied with the treatment meted out to them, might do well to consult a broker. He will advise and certainly cut down the legwork. Beware his asking any fee. If money is mentioned for the services he proposes on your behalf, make for the door! His commission comes from the other side and he is not entitled to it from you as well.

Institutional lenders do not all view properties in the same light. For example, in towns where predominantly properties are very old, usually dating between 1880 and 1910 as in many of the country's major Industrial Revolution towns in the Midlands and North, a purely local building society will be much more inclined to lend than one of the big national societies. Other lenders are beginning to call 1930s properties 'old' and are less inclined to advance more than 85 to 90 per cent of their valuation of a house. There are also differing treatments in the types of accommodation; houses and bungalows usually are comparable. Period properties, which might have been built at any time from the 13th to the 18th or early 19th centuries can be difficult when it comes to qualifying for large mortgages. Some building societies prefer not to touch them at all; some will give advances of perhaps 75 per cent, a few may go to 80, others not above 50 per cent. Often an assurance company, with special protection by way of an endowment policy to cover the amount of a mortgage is a better bet. Much the same goes for a country cottage, although well-placed and well-modernized specimens can often qualify for a maximum loan of 90 per cent. Again, much depends upon the attitude and policy of a society.

In the case of pre-1919 housing, local authorities turn out to be the major lenders. They have, these days, the attitude that many of the older terraces of two- and three-bedroom homes, built about and before the turn of the century, are better modernized and retained than demolished and replaced. In conjunction with their lending policies, which, however, are subjected to the vagaries of the economy from time to time, local authorities today endeavour to encourage revitalization of older areas and do their part by laying out open spaces and areas of greenery. As well as mortgages, local authorities are empowered to give grants to bring elderly homes up to date with the installation of essential services.

For many years, building societies shied away from providing mortgages on flats and maisonettes and many still do. Where flats constitute a major sector of a particular locality, societies have relented but again, local societies are usually more amenable than the bigger outside societies. None of them very much likes a flat in a converted house and all want a definite clause stipulating that there is responsibility for common areas in blocks of flats, notably the corridors, party walls, entrance halls and so on, and the amount of mortgage very much depends upon how tightly the responsibility for these is drawn up. It might be possible, in the case of conversions to find a private mortgage, possibly through a solicitor or accountant, and if so, the likelihood would be that it would only be granted at a comparatively high rate of interest. The same may be true in the case of the period property in

29

which a building society or assurance company shows little or no interest.

Housing associations

Since the war several attempts at some form of cooperative building and buying have been made. Promoters discovered that such forms of development rarely worked out less expensively than could have been executed by normal private building operations. Under recent legislation, housing associations and cooperatives which previously had schemes for rent/co-ownership, mainly in blocks of flats, have scarcely become much more than an adjunct to the local authorities which in practice nominate tenants considered suitable for this form of accommodation. The principle of selection is based on providing a home for those who fall between eligibility for a council house and inability to purchase a place of their own.

In any event, foundation members of housing associations discovered successively that, as time went on, they were unable to execute projects as cheaply, let alone less expensively, than builders and developers well skilled in mass construction work. Costs therefore had squeezed housing association programmes out of the reach of those at whom they were aimed and co-ownership has largely fizzled out insofar as new work is concerned, though of course, the earlier schemes are still being operated. Now housing associations are overseen by the Government-sponsored Housing Corporation which is responsible for promoting, supervising and funding them. The Housing Corporation however, does supply finance for groups of people wanting to build their own homes. The self-build principle is based on the combination of a number of prospective owners joining together and pooling their skills, knowledge, abilities and experience. They build homes for themselves and each other on a chosen site, all working through until the last person involved is able to move into his completed home. Usually, when homes are erected on the self-build principle, normal building society mortgages are taken out so that the group's debt to the Housing Corporation may be erased. Each individual then becomes a normal owner-occupier.

Since the end of the last war, when private building started up again after the austerity of the 1939–45 hostilities and subsequent rationing of almost everything, including development, the pattern of house-building, buying and selling changed somewhat. Because of the shortage of building land and its ever-increasing cost, developers introduced flats for sale, which, along with what were called mews or town houses, that is, homes in modern terraces, sometimes on three floors, provided some innovation. Up till then, few flats had ever been offered for sale, though there had been many blocks, particularly in London and in Scottish towns, to rent.

Lately some local authorities have introduced a 'fifty-fifty' rent/purchase scheme. Under this procedure, a council encourages occupiers of its properties to become owners by partly renting and partly buying a house. In this respect Birmingham Corporation were the pioneers and, as well as reducing the subsidies required for council housing, the system is considered to be an economic method of creating home ownership. Occupiers meet the cost of management and maintenance as they would do as owners in any event. There have also been isolated cases of private builders operating a similar rent/buy scheme. Under their procedure, a house was available at a figure per week judged by the builder as being capable of being upheld by the prospective occupant. Of that figure, say £10 a week, half was retained as rent by the builder, the balance was put into a building society on behalf of the occupant. When the building society money had been accumulated to the point where it was sufficient for the occupant to 'put down' as a deposit for purchase this was done and the occupant became again an owner-occupier in the normal way.

It is true to say that virtually every house these days is bought with the help of a loan. A major attraction is that there is tax relief on loans up to a limit of £25,000, so that even if a buyer does not necessarily need the purchase money it is often to his advantage to take out a mortgage to ease his liability for tax.

Throughout Britain, 54 per cent of the population is in owner-occupied accommodation, compared with an average of 46·6 per cent a decade or so ago. The highest number of owner-occupiers is in Wales where more than 58 per cent are in their own homes. In England the percentage is 55, and in Scotland, where there has been a long tradition of renting via local authority estates, 33·5. In the mid-1960s, the percentage of owners in Wales was 52, in England 48· 5 and in Scotland 28·5.

In broad terms, the highest rate of owner-occupation is in the London area and the Home Counties, which have a long history of home-buying. Huge estates were created before the last war, mainly in the late 1920s and 1930s, built to accommodate those who travelled up to 30 and more miles to and from work in the City and West End. As one goes north, the numbers of owners generally decrease, though in recent years, because they had a great deal of leeway to make up, these other regions are now among the leaders in house purchase. Apart from house price levels generated in London and to a lesser extent by those set in other major conurbations like the Midlands, Merseyside and, in Scotland, the capital, Edinburgh, other factors can also arise. These include demand for second homes in special areas noted for their beauty and general amenities. This demand fluctuates according to the whims of the day, the incidence of taxation and the cost of maintaining another establishment.

2

HOW TO GO ABOUT IT

Before making any major move about a particular property there should be a clear indication of just what is involved. Houses and flats may be freehold or leasehold, subject to a ground rent or to a chief rent, or, in Scotland, a feu duty. Properties may be registered or unregistered. It is necessary to find out exactly where any house or flat offered fits in to these categories and what is involved in the way of payments. Obviously, ground rents are payable every year until the end of a lease, chief rents, which are ground rents in another form, are payable in perpetuity. Freeholds have no such annual payments but there may be covenants on them which preclude owners from doing certain things or make it a condition of doing certain other things. For example, there are properties on private estates which lay down rules about the types of houses which may be built, their styles and costs. It is also probable that in such cases there is an annual charge for the maintenance or building of roads and services. The latter may include wages for a porter, a gardener or some other employee whose job it is to see that standards are met and kept.

Leases often stipulate terms about the upkeep of a property and normally these are not very onerous. Generally they amount to little more than good housekeeping. A typical clause might lay down that the exterior should be painted at intervals of not less than five years or that the premises must not be used for obnoxious or undesirable trades.

Terms used in connection with changes of ownership of properties vary according to the category of the house or flat. They all mean much the same thing, but the acquisition of a lease involves what is legally referred to as an assignment; a change of ownership of a registered house is called a transfer and where an unregistered house is involved, the legal process is carried out by way of a conveyance.

Leases on houses and flats are for stated terms. In the case of flats these terms vary and can be from as low as 50 years to 999 years. Freehold means that there is no such limit. Again, in general, a freehold will be more expensive than a leasehold, a house which is registered is more easily, that is less costly, transferred than one which is unregistered. That is because the latter investigation of the title, or ownership, involves more work in checking.

In the case of registered property, descriptions are maintained about ownership at the Land Registry, along with pertinent details. That means that there is little complication about finding out what is relevant to a sale or purchase. Unregistered land however, indicates there is no such easy way of checking and a seller is bound to prove ownership. This he does by producing deeds or other papers which embrace transactions over the past 15 or 20 years. It is on this information that what is called an abstract of title is procured and a purchaser is required to check, or have checked, the line of ownership which finishes with the seller.

It is as well to remember that, where a buyer is considering applying for a loan to help him purchase his home, that lending institutions, the building societies, assurance companies and local authorities react in different ways to different types of property. In recent years, building societies have been loath to advance moneys to purchase new homes which are not granted a certificate by the former National House-Builders Registration Council, now called the National House-Building Council. The Council in effect, guarantees a buyer against bad workmanship and ensures in theory at least, that there is redress in both financial and restoration terms, for an aggrieved party. In the case of new homes, building societies and assurance companies will often be prepared to advance on mortgage up to 95 per cent of the total price. Frequently builders and developers have special arrangements with societies for making advances to buyers of their houses.

Viewing

House-hunting can be fun . . . or a chore, depending upon the individual and it should be remembered that everything seems better in the sun! The aim therefore should be to have a look at things in the off-season, in the rain or snow if possible and nothing reveals defects like a good storm and its aftermath! There is nothing sinister in this approach to purchasing a home. After all, a buyer, having paid out substantially for a property, wants least of all to be faced with necessary repairs immediately he has shut the front door behind him. Sun therefore, can be a gay deceiver and rain and wind are welcome suitors. There is little to be concealed in the winter months when buildings stand out stark against the leafless landscape, gardens are at their drabbest and the whole aspect is rather uninviting. If you like the house under those conditions, you'll revel in it when the sunshine strikes! More to the point is that when things are at their gloomiest, a potential buyer can get the best impression not only of a particular house but also of the neighbourhood and its shortcomings, if any (like waiting for a bus which declines to arrive).

Try and look at things before the lights go up. These, like the sun, smooth off the sharp edges and tone down the defects. Start out early in a howling gale and get to a house or flat in mid-morning in a downpour, snowstorm, frost or all three. There is nothing like such a combination for showing up the condition of paths and roads in residential districts and quick-clearing water if observed, is a feather in the cap of the local authority. The elements soon indicate how the house is standing up to them. Clues as to the need or otherwise for repairs and renovations are easily followed. Frost soon uncovers those cement-washed fronts where cracks have allowed moisture to penetrate between bricks and rendered finishes with the resultant unpleasant peeling-off pattern. Unless attended to very promptly there is certainly the basis for a hefty replastering job before damp penetrates the inside walls.

Few surveyors can find entries for their records as quickly as rain can discover them in a bad roof. It soon manages to soak into every nook and cranny and will certainly seep through roof flashings where the lead has come away or is porous through age. Blocked gutter pipes and choked gutters as well as badly-fitting ones are soon brought fully into the glare of public gaze. There is often a nice line to be seen on sagging roofs after a moderate snowfall. Such a situation demands a full-scale inspection of the timbers before there is complete collapse. Inside too, damp very soon makes its mark, irrespective of attempts at concealment and the winter is the time to watch out for it. In upper rooms, damp can indicate a bad roof or, possibly badly-fitting or maybe rotting, window frames. In walls at ground level it could mean a lack of a proper damp course, or none at all. Sometimes it can be caused by sheer thoughtlessness or ignorance, perhaps by an enthusiastic gardener piling soil on his rockery higher than the damp-course or by the malfunctioning of an air brick. Some people, to cut out draughts and to 'improve' insulation have had air bricks removed altogether or have plastered over them. Remember too, that that pleasant walk to a bus stop or station in summer, can be transformed during winter and the slope which, bathed in mellow sunshine during June can become a formidable gradient in February's howling gales. It could be the factor which decides a buyer for or against!

The first steps in buying

Don't rush it. That's the first rule. Do everything methodically and deliberately and keep a constant check on everything. Having decided on the price you can afford and having found a house or flat considered suitable which falls within your means, it is a good idea to put down a holding deposit.

First however, if you do not have a solicitor, and feel you need one, get one. People who have used the services of a solicitor will be ready to advise you to whom to go, or should you wish to choose your own, there are lists to be found in local libraries or in the Law List. In any event, the party from whom you are buying, whether it is a builder, development company or private individual, will require a name so that their solicitor can communicate with him about the purchase.

If you found your house through an estate agent he may suggest your putting down a deposit, and indeed the seller's solicitor is likely to ask you for one anyway. If your solicitor agrees, then lodge a deposit which might be anything from £100 to five per cent of the agreed purchase price but be sure to make it 'subject to contract'. It might be advisable to borrow the deposit from a bank if all your savings are with a building society. Most bank managers are sympathetic in such cases, though they will expect the loan to be cleared off when the purchase is completed.

Nothing should be signed before your solicitor gives the go-ahead, no matter how pressing the other parties are or how enthusiastic you are to see the whole business finished! If up to this point, you have not appointed a solicitor to act for you, be sure that everything you deposit is marked 'subject to contract'. This safeguards you in the event that you do not wish to go farther with your purchase for one reason or another and ensures that any moneys paid will be returned to you. Receipts are important, get them for everything! Up to the deposit stage, nothing except your cheque should be signed! The magic words 'subject to contract' should be stressed in every communication, not because it is most people's intention not to complete a deal, but just in case circumstances arise which make it impossible. The seller has equal rights to pull out too; he may be confronted with unexpected complications.

Meantime, contact should have been made with your building society branch, taking to the manager details of the property you are intending to acquire, and settling the amount of mortgage the society is likely to give. The building society is unlikely to be specific at this stage. The manager will arrange for the property to be surveyed to ensure that it is a good investment. Really the society wants to safeguard its money by making certain that the property is worth at least the amount of the loan proposed.

It is wise for a buyer to have a survey of his own done by a qualified valuer, or architect if preferred, so that defects which might be present can be pointed out. This can be money well spent and a survey should be commissioned as early in the proceedings as possible. Though the surveyor, estate agent or architect carrying out a survey will charge a fee, if there is necessary work to be done, the fact could possibly be used as an excuse to approach the seller for a reduction in his price.

In due course, the building society will tell you how much the advance will be and will set out the terms of repayment. Your solicitor should then be instructed to proceed with the remaining legal formalities which include drawing up the contract. Before that however, he will conduct what are known as 'searches'. These are inquiries to elucidate whether or not there are impediments to the sale. He will ask the local council about any plans it might have for road widening or compulsorily acquiring land or for other works which might affect the property in question. If there are probable developments which are considered hazards for the future, you might wish to withdraw from the proposed sale. As you will not have signed any agreement, document or other legal paper or contract up to this stage, you will be free to do so. During this time, the seller's solicitor will have had prepared and sent to your solicitor a draft contract. This is only prepared after the deeds to the property or copies of them, have been obtained. The deeds are important because, like a car registration book they disclose the history of the property and the right of the seller to sell it.

Climax is reached when, all snags having been ironed out, it is time for contracts to be signed and exchanged. The seller signs one and the buyer the other. In the contract will be a number of details, including when the sale is to be completed, that is, when the buyer has paid over the money and the house becomes his. It will also signify the amount paid by way of a deposit. Once signed and exchanged the contracts are binding on both parties and the buyer is expected to lodge a deposit equal to 10 per cent of the full purchase price, less the sum of any initial deposit. As the house is now the buyer's, even if he is not yet living in it, insurance should be taken out to cover its value.

There remain other important documents, the conveyance or transfer or the assignment. These where appropriate will be signed by the seller and acquired by the purchaser's solicitor. They do what they imply, give ownership to the purchaser. Normally, before a buyer's solicitor asks for a signature he will set in motion a further investigation to satisfy himself that everything is in order from the purchasing angle. Coordination has been the key up to this point. Behind the scenes, as it were, papers about the mortgage will have been received from the building society or assurance company or local authority, all to be signed and meanwhile a meeting will have been arranged between the seller's solicitor, the building society, assurance company or local authority and the purchaser so that what is known as 'completion' can take place. At the meeting the buyer's solicitor will require the moneys necessary to bridge the gap between what is being loaned by way of mortgage and what has been deposited already and while it all sounds very complicated and formidable it is mainly carried on by solicitors via letters or phone calls as far as the buyer and seller are concerned.

One final communication is likely to inform a buyer that he has become a legal owner, but of course, as a security for the loan, the lender retains possession of the deeds and other relevant papers until such time as the mortgage is redeemed. There are variations on this method of buying. For instance a purchaser may not require a mortgage so that there is no need for building societies to intervene. In such cases solicitors acting between the parties prepare the necessary documents and arrange for payment of the sums of money involved, setting out

36

clearly any special considerations about the transaction.

As the onus is always on purchasers to ensure that they know what they are buying, they can't be too careful. Better safe than sorry even if it costs something to be certain. Far too few people bother to have a proper survey done of the house they propose to purchase before they sign on the dotted line. That can be a costly omission. Surveys are invaluable to ascertain that the house on which a buyer has set his heart (and proposes to set his life savings and earnings) is up to scratch. A survey can be put in hand simply by asking a building surveyor to go over the property professionally so that any defects may be pinpointed. It is a well-known and acknowledged fact that a house-buyer, at the point of buying, is fully stretched financially, but that should not rule out his putting aside £75 to £130 for a survey to ensure that what he is buying is perfectly sound or has only minor faults which can easily be put right.

Finding a surveyor is also relatively easy. Most estate agents firms have a building surveyor on their staffs or are able to call upon a qualified person who is able to conduct a professional survey. It is an added safeguard if the person so appointed is a member of the Royal Institution of Chartered Surveyors or the Rating and Valuation Association, Faculty of Architects and Surveyors, or of the Incorporated Society of Valuers and Auctioneers. They may be recognized by the letters FRICS or ARICS in the case of members of the Royal Institution and FSVA or ASVA in the case of the Incorporated Society. These bodies, along with the National Association of Estate Agents, MNAEA, also have bonding arrangements which protect members of the public who wish to deposit moneys with them during the course of house purchasing. What must be borne in mind is that houses are built of a number of volatile materials, some of which, especially in newer buildings, have not proved themselves over a lengthy period yet and so are liable to act or react in certain ways due to violent changes in temperature or weather. Truth to tell there are few, if any really perfect buildings about, however new or old they are. What a building surveyor has is an eye trained to spot defects which an enthusiastic purchaser may well easily overlook, as well as knowing where to look for specific faults such as wet and dry rot, cracking, bad plumbing and so on.

Remember when seeking a surveyor that not all estate agents are qualified surveyors and not all surveyors are in business as estate agents selling houses.

Making the preliminary moves costs nothing and a discussion about the house it is proposed to buy with a surveyor will indicate to him what he might have to look for. Certain areas are prone to dry rot for example and a local surveyor will know this and look for signs of it. At this point too, agreement should be made over the fee to be paid which will rarely be more than £250 for an ordinary house. Even if the survey reveals that everything is all right (though it would seldom be the case that a surveyor would not find some item which would be better dealt with) the fee paid is worth it in peace of mind knowing that there are no major defects to be remedied. Not all surveyors or people who call themselves surveyors, are qualified, so that is a point to watch and it may be to a purchaser's advantage to look around a few firms or individuals to decide which one will give best value for money.

What a buyer spends on his survey actually depends on how detailed he wishes the survey to be. Looking over floors instead of under the floorboards is obviously less costly; looking at plumbing and drains is cheaper than having them thoroughly tested and so on. As a rule of thumb; the older the building the more detailed should be the survey. It may be a fact that the building has stood the test of time till now but you don't want it to end its useful life at your expense!

It will not be possible to count on any building society which is going to advance a mortgage on a particular house providing you, as buyer, with a copy of the surveyor's report which it commissions for its own guidance. The building society merely wishes to have an assurance that the structure is sound and that it will get its money back in the event of having to foreclose on the borrower. At the same time the borrower must meet the cost of the building society survey as part of the condition of getting his mortgage. Another point is that, should a surveyor for a building society fail to report a fault, there would not be a case against him for negligence which could be followed up by the buyer. That is where the personally-commissioned survey differs; the buyer does have redress in the event of negligence by the surveyor. Complaints are handled through the professional bodies which is why it is sensible to ensure that any building surveyor commissioned is a member of one or other of them.

As for the money to pay for such surveys, very few bank managers are so hard-hearted as to refuse a loan for a short period to meet the cost. There never is any harm in asking for one and the worst he can say is 'No'. If he does, try another bank! They're all out for business like every other commercial organization and all bank managers are different and view requests differently too. There are no scale fees for this type of survey. Neither the Royal Institution of Chartered Surveyors nor the Incorporated Society of Valuers and Auctioneers has found it practicable to prepare one. The fee would depend not only on the age of the property but also on its general state; for example, if a surveyor finds dry rot in one corner of a room he may have to remove many floor boards to discover the full extent of the damage. It is almost impossible, therefore, to judge the amount of time a survey would take merely from the price of the house. But, as a general guide, £150 to £250 should be the maximum for the average house.

Sometimes it is possible to be a purchaser when a landlord agrees to sell a house or flat to a sitting tenant. Normally this is a straightforward transaction though the purchaser's solicitor will make intensive searches again to ensure that the property is the landlord's to sell and to clear any particular clauses which may have been inserted when the property was first let. A sitting tenant with a good record usually has very little trouble obtaining a loan to help him purchase and the completion is so smooth that one week he is paying rent, the next he has become the owner. Loans are available from the same sources; building societies, assurance companies and local authorities.

Borrowing the money

Having decided which property to buy, and where applicable nominated a solicitor to act, a mortgage application form should be obtained from a building society chosen. This will require details of the loan sought and should be returned to the society's office together with the appropriate inspection fee. It is customary for societies to take up references with employers to confirm details of income. When these formalities have been gone through, the building society will send a valuer to inspect the property concerned and he will report his findings to the society, not to the purchaser or seller. In due course the society will notify its offer. Often it is possible for a buyer to obtain a separate report from the same surveyor on payment of a percentage of his normal charge.

It cannot be over-emphasized that those planning to borrow to buy a house should consult a building society about prospects as early as possible. A chat with the local manager or other official of a society can be most helpful. There is little point in wasting time and money inspecting properties which are too expensive against the amount likely to be available by way of a loan.

It is often sound advice to go to a local building society if there is one. Alternatively, the big societies have offices in many towns throughout the country. It is also possible to find out from the Building Societies' Association a list of suitable societies and there are other societies which have been granted 'trustee status' by the Government. The Building Societies' Year Book, which may be consulted at libraries and sometimes at estate agents' offices, gives complete details of all societies.

Questions always arise over how much may be borrowed. The amount depends upon the financial status of the applicant and repayments are usually worked out so that it costs the borrower no more per month than his income per week. With a mortgage rate of 14½ per cent, slightly more or less, most societies will advance 2½ times the gross yearly earnings of an applicant and some part of a wife's income may also be taken into account. On the question of price, a society will normally lend up to 80 per cent of the value of a house or its purchase price, whichever is the lower. Should the amount to be borrowed be higher than that, say up to 95 per cent, the applicant will be required to provide some form of additional security. This is usually in the form of a guarantee by an assurance company for which a single premium will have to be paid. Often this is added to the loan and repaid over the life of the mortgage.

Providing the rules are followed, house buying in Britain is a fairly simple operation. Unlike in America, 100 per cent mortgages are the exception rather than the rule and finance corporations such as exist abroad rarely handle house purchase in this country. Building societies are the main sources of finance for house buying and they normally require a deposit from a borrower of 5 to 15 per cent and sometimes more, depending upon status. To borrow £10,000 an applicant would need a yearly income of at least £4,000 and repayments on that sum would cost about £130 a month gross for a 20 year term. But, because of his necessity to meet the ratio of income to monthly repayments a borrower would really require a yearly salary closer to £5,000. On his £4,000 income he would be restricted to about an £8,000 advance, costing around £104 a month.

Whether or not the income of a working wife is taken into account varies with the policies of the different societies. Some take a third of a wife's earnings into account; others may allow half. Some again, with faith in the Pill and the word of the applicant that there will be no family, may allow the full amount to count towards a loan.

There is in addition no guarantee that the property for which a loan is sought will be valued at the same figure as its selling price. Building societies conduct their own surveys for the purpose of deciding values and these are really based on what the particular house involved would bring were the applicant for a loan to default and the property have to be sold. Societies wish to ensure that their loans are adequately covered for all eventualities! A major factor taken into account is the age of the property and most building societies prefer modern houses, which include generally those built since the 1930s, and it is fairly safe to work on the principle that the newer the building the higher the loan, all other things being equal. Well-modernized and maintained older houses will of course, also qualify though advances will possibly be restricted to perhaps between 50 to 80 per cent of the lender's valuation of the property.

To help borrowers who are unable to obtain tax relief on their mortgage interest because they are not eligible for income tax at the standard rate, the Government introduced the Option Mortgage Scheme some years ago. It is designed to provide a borrower with a subsidy of sorts. When the normal interest rate on a mortgage is between 14 and 14·6 per cent, this subsidy represents 3·6 per cent on the outstanding debt, or 4·05 per cent where a loan has been arranged in conjunction with an endowment assurance policy. In practice, a loan at 14·5 per cent is reduced by tax considerations to 10·15—10·85 per cent. The home-buyer pays this to the society and the society draws the balance from the Government. An extension of the Option Mortgage Scheme can be used to provide 100 per cent mortgages on the value of a house. In such cases a small single premuim will be necessarily paid to an assurance company. Borrowers of course, still have to be able to repay the monthly sums equivalent to not more than a week's income.

For those liable to income tax at the standard rate, mortgage interest ranks for relief. This is given through the normal pay-as-you-earn channels. If it is paid out of earned income, at the standard rate, 14 per cent mortgage means an effective rate of 10·15 per cent.

Changes in the standard rate of income tax or the interest rate on loans obviously affect these figures but the percentages are maintained so that the relief granted by an Option Mortgage is in practice equivalent to that given through normal mortgage arrangements.

In its earliest stages the option mortgage was limited to £7,000 but the limit was later raised to £25,000. The rate varies with the interest payable on the ordinary repayment mortgage and the idea behind the scheme is to put the option mortgagor and the normal borrower on an equal footing with the latter claiming tax relief. If a person's income is likely to rise the option mortgage is not a proposition. If an income is likely to fall, say a working wife stops work when a family comes along, then the option mortgage could be worth while. An advantage with an option mortgage is that a borrower may be able to obtain 100 per cent of the valuation of a house. That valuation however, is the one placed on a house by the building society and not by the seller, so the two may differ considerably. The wider the gap in these instances and the lower the percentage of the price advanced by the society the more a buyer has to find by way of a deposit.

Tax relief is given on mortgages up to a limit of £25,000. The relief is on the interest only, not the capital; so monthly repayments include interest and some capital, any tax relief falls progressively over the years as the amount of capital left to pay off falls and in consequence, the amount of interest to be paid on what is remaining also decreases. There are variations which include low-start mortgages where repayments increase as the years pass and the option mortgages which are at a lower level as tax relief is embodied in the repayments. Option mortgages are suitable for a person whose tax liabilities do not put him into brackets where he pays the standard rates. In the case of mortgages granted through assurance companies allied with an endowment insurance policy tax relief is given on both the annual interest payable on the loan and the amounts payable for the insurance. The relief is constant as far as the income tax rate is constant, for the whole term of the loan.

An indication of how the tax relief affects borrowers is provided by the following table:

TABLE 1

(i)	(ii)	(iii)	(iv)	(v)	(vi)	(vii)
			Option Mortgage Scheme			
Rate of Mortgage Interest	Tax Relief at 30%	Net Rate of Interest	Annuity or Fixed Instalment Mortgages		Endowment or Standing Mortgages	
			Subsidy	Rate Paid	Subsidy	Rate Paid
%	%	%	%	%	%	%
11·00	3·30	7·70	3·30	7·70	3·05	7·95
11·50	3·45	8·05	3·50	8·00	3·25	8·25
11·75	3·52	8·23	3·50	8·25	3·25	8·50
12·00	3·60	8·40	3·50	8·50	3·25	8·75
12·50	3·75	8·75	3·70	8·80	3·45	9·05
13·00	3·90	9·10	3·90	9·10	3·65	9·35
13·50	4·05	9·45	4·10	9·40	3·85	9·65
14·00	4·20	9·80	4·10	9·90	3·85	10·15
14·50	4·35	10·15	4·30	10·20	4·05	10·45
15·00	4·50	10·50	4·50	10·50	4·25	10·75
15·50	4·65	10·85	4·50	11·00	4·25	11·25
16·00	4·80	11·20	4·50	11·50	4·25	11·75
16·50	4·95	11·55	4·50	12·00	4·25	12·25

Information supplied by the Building Societies Association.
The table above gives a comparison of the reliefs and net rates paid on a range of mortgage interest rates. The tax relief figures in column (ii) are those for 1970/80 and the option subsidy rates in columns (iv) and (vi) apply from September 1, 1979.

Most banks also have Home Mortgage schemes; the following table illustrates the monthly repayments per £1000 borrowed, currently offered by Barclays Bank.

TABLE 2

Interest rate	10 years £	15 years £	20 years £	25 years £
9	12·63	10·10	8·95	8·34
10	13·16	10·69	9·59	9·02
11	13·71	11·30	10·25	9·72
12	14·27	11·92	10·92	10·44
13	14·84	12·56	11·61	11·17
14	15·42	13·20	12·31	11·91
15	16·01	13·86	13·03	12·66
16	16·61	14·54	13·75	13·42

The precise monthly repayment figure for any particular mortgage amount would be assessed more precisely than is possible from the above table, which only gives a guide.

Mortgage rates fluctuate and are generally geared to changes in the Government's official lending rates, although not directly linked with them. Building societies have to compete with other investment media and therefore have to offer their investors a return in line with those available to savers from other forms of investment.

As interest rates rise, building societies are forced to fall in line, with the result that those who have borrowed on mortgage are asked to pay more. In some cases when a rise occurs, the particular society will allow the borrower to extend the term of his loan but, as can be seen from the following table, it is not always possible for the term to be extended.

TABLE 3

Term in years	Monthly repayment at 10¼ per cent interest rate on £1,000 loan £	Monthly repayment at 12¼ per cent interest rate on £1,000 loan £	Extended term
5	22·27	23·27	5 yrs 3 mths
10	13·36	14·90	11 yrs 6 mths
15	11·28	12·40	20 yrs 4 mths
20	10·13	11·34	Infinity
25	9·54	10·81	Infinity
30	9·22	10·54	Infinity
35	9·03	10·40	Infinity

Once the term of loan becomes infinite, the society will insist that the borrower increases the level of payment.

TABLE 4

Amount of loan £	Repayments at 12 per cent £	Repayments at 14 per cent £	Rise £
5,000	55·80	62·95	7·15
10,000	111·60	125·90	14·30
15,000	167·40	188·85	21·45
20,000	223·20	251·80	28·60

For mortages of 20 years

It has been found desirable for those having loans to meet their higher costs rather than extend the terms while keeping payments the same, as in some cases the loans would never be paid off.

Some building societies offer a guaranteed return of between 0·50 per cent and 2·5 per cent above the society's prevailing investment share rate. They offer investors who invest capital with a society for a fixed period of two to five years an extra percentage if capital is left with the society for the whole period. This is equivalent to either 10·25 per cent net for a two-year investment or 11·25 per cent for five years.

In deciding which type of borrowing is best suited to the individual's personal circumstances, there are many aspects to be considered. Underlying the types of endowment mortgages, some without profits and some with, is the basic principle that a loan is issued by an assurance company with an insurance policy to cover the amount. The interest rate for the loan is fixed, and the repayments run in equal amounts for the full term of the mortgage, unlike a straight building society advance which decreases over the years as capital is paid off, and therefore, interest too diminshes. That of course, also reduces the tax relief allowed on interest payments. In the case of an endowment mortgage, tax relief and the tax advantage on the actual payments made for the insurance part of the deal, remain constant throughout the whole tenure of the mortgage.

It has been calculated that the total cost of a £10,000 building society mortgage over 25 years and including a mortgage protection policy for a man of 34 at the interest rate of 11 per cent is £23,540 after taking into consideration tax relief at 35 per cent. There is by comparison, a total cost of £22,983 for a non-profit endowment policy mortgage costing £76·61 a month.

There is also to be taken into consideration the fact that, if prices follow their usual pattern, the capital value of the house on which the mortgage is held will have gone up. So, it is again a case of 'you takes your chance and makes your choice'. Most people will take on what they can afford which gives them the best protection should accident or death intervene. Insurance is a flexible service and there are many companies in the field with schemes which can be tailored to suit an individual's needs.

There are also schemes which provide mortgages to be paid off at variable rates. These are available to borrowers who have jobs where annual salary increments are paid. Mortgage repayments start at lower levels, then rise as incomes rise to meet them. Local and national government officers and professional people such as teachers and lecturers can usually find such schemes to their advantage.

On a £15,000 house a down payment is likely to be between £750 and £1,500. There is a right for option mortgage borrowers to switch to a normal type of mortgage after four years. Whether or not that is to the advantage of the borrower depends upon his income and upon his tax situation over that period of time.

Assurance companies which have schemes based on life insurance are numerous. Again, an assurance or mortgage broker will advise which is the most suitable of scores of methods. Much depends upon the liability for income tax of the applicant for a loan. Some schemes provide much more immediate tax relief; others are of benefit in the longer term.

Among the many is the Low-Cost mortgage plan. After tax relief it works out about the same or possibly a little under the building society repayment method. At the end however, there can be a tax-free lump sum. A With Profits Endowment method involves larger monthly repayments but again the lump sum at the end, also tax-free, can be very much bigger. A straightforward Endowment on the other hand, wipes out, after a stated term, the amount of the loan without providing lump-sum payments at the end. Throughout the term there is tax relief on the interest payable and on the insurance policy. Some finance houses and banks will also make house-purchase loans but for very much shorter periods than the assurance companies and building societies.

Banks also play a part for they can supply what are known as bridging loans. These are advances made by banks to help sellers and purchasers of homes while their finances are being sorted out, enabling them to do exactly what their name implies, bridge the gap between what a person has and what he may expect when negotiations are completed. A bridging loan enables amounts to be drawn to cover essential and immediate outgoings and is given with the expectation when everything is settled, that it will be repaid. Interest is charged on bridging loans in the usual way at the rate current at the time.

Insurance companies also tend to charge slightly higher interest rates on their mortgages than are in force generally at the time they are taken out. They invariably stipulate that loans are made at fixed interest rates which in practice means that a borrower stands to gain or lose if interest charges go up or down. The system however, appeals to those in higher income-tax brackets as they qualify for tax relief both on the insurance and on the mortgage payments. Under an assurance company scheme, unlike building society procedures, the capital remains intact and only the interest is paid monthly or quarterly until the insurance policy matures to wipe out the amount borrowed. With a building society the borrower pays off monthly some capital and the interest.

There are also schemes for lending by local authorities. Normally, councils advance money to selected applicants only. They are generally those who for one or another reason have been turned down by a building society. They may not qualify for the amount sought because their incomes are not sufficiently high or they may wish to acquire a type of property which building societies would rather not touch.

Societies have a leaning towards modern houses and prefer properties built no earlier than the 1920s. Again, councils will generally charge an interest rate above the going rate at the time and again it is usual for them to ask borrowers to agree to the rate being fixed for the full term. On the other hand, a council might very well agree to advance 100 per cent of its valuation of a property while building societies and assurance companies seldom provide more than 90 per cent. Remember always that advances made are given on the basis of the lenders' assessment of what a property is worth, not the asking price.

The later stages

Although it is usual for those seeking a house to peruse the lists maintained by house agents and to sift through advertisements, an alternative is to commission an agent to act. In such cases he will require a fee for his services. Fees, since an Act of Parliament ruled that scales laid down by the various institutions to which agents belong are illegal, should be agreed between an applicant and an agent before he is commissioned to act. Where an applicant seeks a house for himself without commissioning an agent his consultations of lists held by agents, as well as copies of particulars they prepare giving details of houses for sale are free. As agents in such cases are acting for the seller the latter is responsible for meeting fees when a sale takes place. Most people preparing to buy a house employ a solicitor. He acts for them in the necessary negotiations to conclude the legal formalities. Agents will usually be prepared to recommend a solicitor should a buyer not know of one and they will also be ready to hunt out possibilities for a loan should one be required. The agent will also have the name of the seller's solicitor with whom the buyer or his solicitor will be put in touch so that they can start the necessary procedures. It is possible, for buyers and sellers who wish to dispense with the services of a solicitor, to carry through the legalities themselves should they so wish and feel competent to do so.

These legal procedures take the place of the notary who is the intermediary in many other countries, including those in Europe, and people from abroad purchasing in Britain find the process unusual to say the least. Because of the shortage of rented accommodation in Britain, people from overseas who are likely to be based here for a year or two invariably find it not only easier, but more profitable to buy. Those who have acquired middle-price homes in the London area even for a short period, have recouped their capital outlay when the time has come for them to sell. They have usually in addition, made a small profit, which, as several have been heard to remark 'certainly beats renting!'.

Though normally what is termed the completion date for a purchase is 28 days after the exchange of contracts, the term can be varied by agreement between buyer and seller. It is not likely that the keys of a property purchased will be available to the buyer until actual completion has taken place, though again there can be an agreement earlier. Sometimes buyers and sellers come to an arrangement for allowing the former in to measure up for curtains and the like and to move in more quickly if there are special circumstances.

Buying should be pursued with selling in mind! A judicious purchase will usually pay off handsomely. Few owners stay in one house all their lives. True there are landed families who have held large houses for generations and who continue to reside in the stately home but for most it is a question of changing up or down as the vicissitudes of life unfold.

There must, then, be arrangements for moving from one house or flat to another and the cost of such moves involves quite considerable sums. Within a short space of time, one property must be sold and another bought without any short cuts in procedure. As costs for everything rise, so does the cost of moving, including the actual packing and transport of furniture which is embodied in any such operation.

Fees, charges, rates and other costs

There are a number of basic costs on the legal side which are inescapable, others which may be kept to a minimum and some which can be considerably lower by 'do-it-yourself' conveyancing. However, do-it-yourself is not for everyone and most will use a solicitor to see them through the legal niceties. Both selling and purchasing charges due to a solicitor can be negotiated just like those of estate agents. A solicitor is entitled to charge what is considered fair and reasonable and in the event of a dispute the Law Society may be called in to arbitrate.

Technically an agent is entitled to a fee for providing a valuation of the property if he is asked to do so, though many waive that charge if they are given the job of selling the property concerned. If, at the same time, an agent is charged with finding another house or flat specifically, he would be justified in requesting a fee for his services in that direction. In practice he may already have on his books a property which could be acceptable to a seller seeking an alternative home in which case there would not be a fee. Agents act for clients, generally the sellers and must be instructed in proper terms if they are to be commissioned to look for a property for a buyer. Purchasers are also responsible for meeting stamp duty fees. These are payable on houses costing above £15,000. See Table 6 on page 133.

Though scale fees for solicitors and estate agents were abolished a few years ago, an indication of the variation of charges made between registered and unregistered property may be judged from them. On a £10,000 house or flat the fee for registered property was £62·50 compared with £105 for unregistered and on a £25,000 home £99·75 against

£180. These payments too, are the purchaser's responsibility, while a seller meets the fees on estate agents' handling of a sale. Many work on a percentage of the price of the house though this may be varied by agreement *before* a commission is given to an agent. Previous scale fees may be used as a guide and on the sale of a £10,000 house these were £212·12, on a £25,000 home £437·50. Several now charge 1½ per cent all through, i.e. £150 on £10,000 to £375 on £25,000. Others work on 2 per cent and some on 2½ per cent. On higher-value homes most will agree a figure for a sale.

Numbers of estate agents as well as brokers, employ specialists in mortgage and financial services departments who are ready to give advice and to obtain loans on behalf of purchasers. They are in touch usually with one or two major building societies and a host of other smaller ones as well as finance houses and their advice is free.

Between the mortgage loan and the house price and various other commitments which are to be met, is the buyers' share, known as the deposit. Apart from amassing a deposit and putting a little by to bridge any possible gap between valuation and purchase price, there are other factors to be taken into account, all of which cost money. First there are fees for a solicitor usually employed to see to all the legal formalities. These do vary considerably, but are based broadly on the price of the property concerned and the amount of work which has to be done to transfer ownership from one party to another. In any event there are some set charges such as stamp duty and those concerning registration, which means that the property being sold is what it purports to be. These charges are between £20 and £30 for homes in the £9,000 to £15,000 bracket. To be catered for also is the survey carried out for a building society, assurance company or council granting a mortgage. This survey is basically a valuation and is for the lenders' own use and is not normally available to an applicant for a loan. He should make provision for a fee for an independent survey which depending upon how detailed it is required to be can cost anything from about £15 to more than £100. The building society or assurance company survey costs £21 for a £10,000 house rising to £51 for a £40,000 property and above that figure the fee is by arrangement with the surveyor carrying out the inspection. At the bottom end £5 is payable for a valuation up to £2,000 while for more than £2,000 but under £15,000 the fee is £5 plus £1 for every £500 or part of £500.

Then there are those incidentals, often forgotten, but ever present once a property is actually bought. Insurance is the responsibility of the purchaser as soon as he is at contract stage, though a solicitor normally looks to this. Moneys however should be set aside for the preliminaries which include the men carrying out a removal – they insist on payment when the job of moving in the furniture is completed – and there are little bits and pieces necessary for initial comfort. Electric plugs for instance can become costly items if they have all to be immediately replaced because sockets are different.

First through the letterbox is undoubtedly likely to be the rates notice. That usually wipes out the satisfied smiles on taking over a new home and removes the gilt of the greeting cards expressing the hope of a happy settling-in! Among major expenses facing all householders is the payment of rates. In recent years, because of the increase in the cost of living, rates have gone up considerably along with everything else, though many argue that they are out of proportion these days compared with other services. Rates are levied by local authorities to meet the costs of facilities such as education, policing, libraries, street cleansing and maintenance and in general seeing to social services affecting the community. Thus, local authorities must meet the expenses of all these items and, just as costs rise for an individual who has to pay for wages and salaries, electricity, gas, transport and so on, so of course they do for councils. In theory rates are assessed on the basis of what a property would fetch as rented accommodation in a *free* market. For many years however, this has been an artificial basis, as, with housing shortages, particularly since the last war along with rent controls which have resulted in fewer places becoming available to let, there has been a complete absence of a free market, when the forces of demand and supply could have uninterrupted play.

As the specific amount of rates payable is calculated on two main considerations; the rateable value of a house and the rate in the pound, it is obvious that these can be subject to change. Indeed, from time to time, (officially it should be every five years) assessments are revised in accordance with the increase (or decrease) of the capital value of a property, so there are changes on occasion to which a householder has a right to object if he considers they are unreasonable.

The rateable value of a house is a figure arrived at by the Inland Revenue's Valuation Officer for the district in which the property is situated. He calculates it from information supplied to him and his assessment is then subject to the local authority's levy based on what it requires to meet its forthcoming bills. This rate in the £ as it is known, is variable from year to year and brings in more (or less) as it goes up (or down). The valuation officer arrives at two separate figures on the basis of information given him as a result of questions which must be answered by a householder. He arrives at what is termed the gross value from which are made deductions covering the necessary costs of maintaining a property in good repair. In the expenses column are items such as insurance and amounts for small repairs. When he has subtracted the total allowance for these items, he arrives at the net rateable value of the house, that is the figure on which the owner will pay his rates. It is on the net rateable value that the local council bases its demand – but not necessarily on the full amount of the rateable value figure. That is where the 'rate in the £' comes in. If for example, a property has a rateable value of £200 and the council levies its demand on a rate in the £ of 50p, then a householder's liability will be for £100. Councils themselves as far as rates are concerned have calls on them and help too; the first from the county in whose region they are situated which asks for and receives a proportion of what the local authority collects and the second in the form of a grant from the Government. Both these are taken into account when assessing the rate in the £.

Rate notices are sent to occupiers stating the amount owing and normally they are payable in advance in half-yearly or quarterly instalments. Some councils allow rates to be paid monthly if it is easier for owners so desiring it to meet the bills that way. Those seeking variation from the normal practice should inquire about alternatives from the local town hall or council office. With the rates are other imposts, including payment for water. Water rates are assessed on a percentage of the rateable value of a house and are levied on that basis. There may be strictly local charges, maybe for special drainage facilities, though recent court cases have now indicated that these are no longer payable. A number of residents enjoying the facilities of a common are also sometimes called upon to meet a small demand for the privilege.

One of the main reasons for an alteration in rateable values is a change of structure. Where additions are made to the property, a fresh valuation will be assessed by the local valuation officer and he knows about such extensions simply because, when planning consents are given for the work, he is informed of the fact. Improvements internally, which might not be known to the valuation officer at one stage are revealed to him when he next requires an owner to answer his questionnaire. Those who consider they have a case for seeking a reduction of rateable values must furnish proof. Generally they must indicate a deterioration in their standard of living caused by factors which have emerged since they arrived and took over the property concerned or they can fight against what they consider is an over-zealous assessment.

In the case of a new property an occupier who considers the assessment too high should appeal immediately the figures are known. There is, of course, a form to be filled in on which the appellant lays down his objections. The form is obtained from the local valuation office. A council official will help if necessary by producing the assessments made on properties nearby if the argument is simply that the valuation suggested is considered excessive. At this point the valuation officer has power to suggest a new figure which may be mutually agreed and that will be the end of the matter. If there is no agreement and both sides are adamant the case goes to a local valuation panel to be treated as an appeal against the valuation officer's assessment. The panel sits in a way similar to ordinary magistrates' court, with evidence taken on oath and is empanelled as necessary, with a chairman and two members. Unless he appoints experts to give evidence for him, and for which they will expect a professional fee, an appeal by a householder to a valuation panel is free. There is a further opportunity to fight on if a person is dissatisfied, by taking the next step, an appeal to the Lands Tribunal and again the only outlay to the appellant is for fees to professional witnesses if any.

People on low incomes who find rates payments a hardship are able to apply for rebates to help. Those who qualify are widowed, separated, divorced or single persons earning less than a stated minimum whose rates are not already accounted for in assistance from supplementary benefits. Proof is required and there are forms to be completed but again, assistance is available from the local rating department and other council housing departments. If in doubt the best advice is to apply.

Sometimes, even in the best-regulated households, owners who are committed to mortgage repayments find that they are unable to maintain them. They may have employment or domestic upsets which interrupt their incomes or change the emphasis on them. Whenever it is found that repayments are a hardship, the building society, insurance company or other institution which advanced the loan should be informed. Most will be sympathetic and suggest alternatives to suit the circumstances. Very few, except in a last resort, will foreclose on the mortgagor and sell the property over his head, although in a number of cases this might be considered the wisest course for all concerned. There are special arrangements where broken marriages have caused a new set of circumstances and these provide safeguards for a deserted wife. Her charter is the Matrimonial Homes Act, 1967 under which a wife or a husband where the wife bought the house, can obtain a court order to occupy the matrimonial home. Legislation ensures that one partner cannot sell the house without the consent of the other. There is provision for legal aid for solicitors' fees which may have to be incurred. Other legislation deals with divorce and judicial separation. Under the Matrimonial Causes Act, 1973 the deserted partner can seek the court's direction that the matrimonial home is transferred to him or her. A wife would, with her children, if any, under those circumstances, qualify for welfare payments to help with her mortgage repayments, as well as with any additional interest which may be payable on second mortgages and for insurance, repairs and rates. Whatever the situation however, the essential first move is to acquaint the mortgagees with the facts of the case so that proper arrangements can be made to meet repayments.

Unfortunately in this life, none of us knows exactly how things are to pan out no matter what precautions are taken. Houses are expensive items and it behoves owners to take care over their insurance so that if there is a mishap there is adequate cover for restoring the status quo. What must never be forgotten is the salient fact that the selling price of a house is not necessarily its cost of replacement. In times of inflation, the labour and materials required to reinstate a damaged building will have rocketed so that the final bill could well be considerably more than an owner had contemplated. Assurance companies are aware of this state of affairs and are conscious that the man-in-the-street finds it difficult to keep abreast at all times of changes in building costs. They therefore have introduced a scheme which, based on the value of a property at a given time will automatically adjust the insurance cover on it as the years pass, with relevant increases in premiums of course. Still that is better than letting the insurance cover lag so far behind that, should misfortune strike (it did recently when there was extensive and unexpected storm damage) there are insufficient funds readily available to rectify any major holes in roof or walls.

A glance through the columns of the local paper or in a nearby estate agent's window will provide a fair guide about values for the type of house an owner has. Better still and wiser, it would be advisable for him to obtain expert advice on the value from a surveyor and valuer in the area. His fee could be well worth spending and won't be much anyway. From time to time, what is called the index of building prices is issued from which may be worked out the cost of replacing a house at so much a square foot. Having obtained that figure, multiply it by the number of square feet in the house and the answer is its value; as a rule of thumb method this will give an idea of what is involved. When insuring, an owner should ignore the value of the site on which the property stands. it is unlikely to be damaged at all say in the event of fire or flood, or, as happens frequently these days, the advent of a heavy runaway lorry through the front window! What is left is the value of the bricks and mortar plus the skill of the workmen who will put them together and in sound shape and who, of course, must be paid. Prices creep up unbeknown to owners. Five years for a house during the 1970s, doubled and in a number of cases almost trebled its cost of replacement so it is as well not to think that tomorrow will do! Tomorrow could be too late. Estimates by the assurance industry have indicated that 65 per cent of all householders are underinsured and that 35 per cent are 'seriously inadequately' covered. Greatest hazards are from storms, fires and break-ins. Assurance companies have what are known as comprehensive policies to take care of such eventualities at a cost of £1·25 per £1,000 always assuming that an owner insures his premises to their full value, otherwise, should some accident occur and the place is considered underinsured, companies will withhold some of the money and pay only a proportion of the total. It works like this – if a person whose house is valued at £30,000 pays insurance on a value of £10,000, any claim he makes is unlikely to be settled for more than a third. Conversely, assurance companies watch for cases where people deliberately overinsure in perhaps the hope that they will reap a handsome benefit. House values which are so hugely enhanced are treated with caution, the companies taking the view that it might be in the insured's mind to stage his own 'accidental' fire.

Though companies' policies vary in some detail, broadly most householders' comprehensive insurance is as comprehensive as the title implies. Covered are buildings for damage by fire, lightning, explosion, earthquake, impact by aircraft, impact by road and rail vehicles, and theft. Also embraced is damage by storm, flood, burst pipes, escape of oil from central-heating systems and malicious damage. Some companies incorporate a rule that the householder must meet the first £15 of damage claimed for. The idea is to prevent them being overwhelmed by minor claims requiring much administrative time and effort but it is possible to find some insurers who will bear claims without the £15 excess clause. The cover given usually also extends to include sheds, greenhouses, gates and fences. Fences however, are rarely covered for damage by storm or flood the view being taken officially that these are often in such a poor state of repair and that maintenance on them has been neglected anyway. Damage to windows, doors, baths, washbasins, sanitary fittings, gas, water and sewage pipes and electricity cables is also seen to and there is also cover for a householder in a case where his buildings might injure a third party. In that event there is a limit on the amount payable. It is either £100,000 or £250,000.

There is little real sympathy in the insurance world for the person who underinsures but expects any claim to be fully met. Take an instance where a man with a £20,000 home insures it for £10,000. He suffers damage of one sort or another costing £100 to rectify. The next year, because of inflation, the same £100 damage costs £125 to repair and so on. In effect the companies contend they can carry only 25 per cent increases in costs without comparable increases in premiums for a very short period. In addition, those policyholders who do keep pace with inflation are in effect subsidizing those who neglect to do so and that is not a situation which the companies have any wish to perpetuate. Hence the underinsured person can expect only undervalue payment for any claim. Though steadily rising values of property have increased assurance company incomes from this source, premiums are little changed from the 1920s when the £1·25 per £1,000 was fixed. At the same time the cost of repairing damage has gone up considerably too since then. An advanage of having an index-linked policy which adjusts values and premiums from year to year is that although a premium falls due to be paid on a particular date, its validity is for a year during which time costs could rise spectacularly but the insured is fully covered for any additional outlay necessary because of this should he suffer damage to his premises.

Separate arrangements are usually made for insuring house contents usually at a rate of £2·50 per £1,000 and several assurers have additional cover to meet other circumstances. For example, some companies will provide for any article stolen or destroyed to be replaced at its new value, disregarding the age of the item. One thinks immediately of carpets in this respect.

Companies differ in detail and on emphasis and where special considerations arise it is frequently sound business to consult a member of the Corporation of Mortgage and Finance Brokers, from whom a list may be obtained. At once there springs to mind the position of properties where the ground is liable to subsidence due to mine workings or other geographical phenomena and a broker can advise on the specialist assurance companies in that field. There are too, policies for landlords who might suffer loss of rent and it is wise to discover which way a company reacts to what is described as 'reasonable' additional expenditure on alternative accommodation should a householder's home be rendered uninhabitable.

Acknowledging the fact that most things are possible at a price most assurance companies will not undertake to include damage by frost. Nor is theft or attempted theft of contents insured if you have loaned or sublet part of your home unless there is proof of forced entry. Excluded too are war risks or contamination by radioactivity from any nuclear fuel or nuclear waste and damage caused by sonic booms. At the same time it is expected that some state agency would take care of such eventualities. Special items of jewellery and other valuables are normally listed and insured separately. Some companies have as an added incentive to use them, free insurance after a certain number of years without a claim. Where this is applicable, a six-year claim-free term usually qualifies for the bonus.

3

SELLING YOUR HOUSE

While there are obligations and expenses relating to house purchase, selling also involves some outlay. This may vary considerably depending upon the method of disposal adopted, but there are inescapable fees and charges, just as in buying.

Many people who, in brighter times, move house, remained absent from the market in the 1970s and among the reasons was simply the cost of actually changing homes. With prices having risen over the years, estate agents' commissions have also risen as these are based on a percentage of the selling figures. To these must be added the solicitors' and other legal fees as well as the cost of the furniture removal men. All these points are weighed against the advantages (and disadvantages) of going to a new place if such a move is not entirely necessary but only desirable from an aesthetic point of view.

Always, of course, the question arises about using an estate agent or not. Perhaps the simplest answer to that is to try selling without one. Many who have attempted the process have either sold for less than they could have obtained because they did not keep up with market trends, or failed to sell at all and in desperation, turned to the estate agent to help. After all, if a sale is not made by him there is no charge; if one is then he is worth his fee.

When it comes to selling, properties conform in a number of respects. Broadly, houses of similar types in similar locations will be only marginally different in price, whatever has been done to tart them up and including if there are any, quite substantial extensions. Though such extensions may have been costly appendages there is no guarantee at all that a buyer will be prepared to pay all that much more just because they are there.

Indeed he may regret them and when the opportunity arises have them removed. Truly, like meat, and poison, one man's additions can become another's subtractions. It is situation which counts most and usually it is the agent who is most experienced at judging how much that is worth in hard cash.

Questions also arise about whether or not and how much, it pays to expend time and money on redecoration, and to execute modest improvements where they are obvious, before putting a place up for sale. Again the advice of an agent can be incalculable and invaluable. A decision can often depend upon the area concerned and the type of purchaser who could be expected to be interested in it. As an example, in the case of a house in a busy community where there is a preponderance of young to middle-aged buyers, the principal attraction could be a less expensive, that is, an undecorated and unimproved place at a lower price than a top-notch, spick-and-span more costly home. Couples may be ready to be do-it-yourselfers to save expense and outgoings especially as is usually the case if the money to purchase is being borrowed and has to be repaid. An elderly couple, say in a south-coast retirement town on the other hand, could well prefer a house or flat ready to walk into without further ado. Such buyers are attracted when they can visualize little upheaval following a move in and are invariably in a position and willing to pay that little bit extra for the privilege. Again, depending upon area and the type of buyer associated with it, there can be important incidentals. Often a good selling point is to offer carpets and curtains. That is not only an attraction but good sense where these items have been specially chosen for the premises. In any event, it seldom pays to lift a fitted carpet as it rarely conforms anywhere else, nor are curtains any better at windows in another place. Agents are handy sources of information about such things and they can also suggest other items best left, maybe plumbed-in washing machines and dishwashers, shower fitments and so on. Even though the modern car is as happy left out in the open as shut up in a garage, the garage is a selling point and many buyers are willing to pay for that facility. Emphasis on this amenity is well worthwhile as it is on a good garden – or lack of one!

Most sellers require to live somewhere else so it is a wise precaution as well as a moneysaver, never to commit oneself to a purchase before one's existing property has been sold. There can be a protective element in the contract of sale to ensure that a vendor is not rendered homeless while looking for a suitable alternative. Ideally an exchange of contracts should take place simultaneously, with the buyer of one house moving in and the seller of that house acquiring his alternative at the same time. Such exchanges are rarely possible except in the case where one or both parties are taking on a property which is new.

Everyone can point to the exceptions which prove the rule, but most agents will be reasonably firm with their clients, the sellers, once a buyer has indicated his desire to purchase. While an agent is duty bound to put all offers received to his clients, he will rarely suggest that they should rule out the bona fide first prospective purchaser. Indeed many decline to continue to handle houses on which an acceptable offer has been made and agreed irrespective of how many other offers are subsequently received. Only in the event of the first person's being unable to complete the deal will the property be re-submitted for sale. Buyers must be given reasonable time to arrange their finances and to inspect the property they wish to purchase. Sellers are under no obligation to point out defects, so that purchasers should be on their guard and the most efficient method is to appoint a surveyor to inspect the property. The cost of his services in this respect is minimal compared with the total cost of the house, and is a wise insurance, with the advantage for the buyer that he may be able to negotiate with the seller taking into account the cost of correcting any faults revealed by the survey. Most sellers are reasonable people and will agree; most will not even know there were defects.

Sellers should have a clear idea of what they are actually offering when they decide to put their houses in the market. Buyers should also be aware of what is included, and what are known as fixtures and fittings should be stated and agreed before a transaction and not removed once the parties have made the deal. In law, unless a sale contract specifically lays down otherwise, a seller is not entitled to remove fixtures and fittings which include broadly everything which is fastened as well as plants and trees in the garden. A seller should indicate to any buyer what is not included in a sale and those items involved should be removed before a new owner takes over. It is obviously dangerous to leave bare electric wires if a fitting is taken down.

There are other points to watch too, when selling. Should a house be left empty before a deal is completed and damage occurs, a seller is likely to be held responsible, as he can be should a property not be properly secured. That is despite the fact that a seller does not guarantee that a property he is selling is in sound condition irrespective of the price. It might be a good idea, though highly unlikely, that a buyer should obtain from a seller some kind of an assurance that a house is in good order. If such an assurance can be obtained in writing then there could be a case for damages if there is an accident or mishap, but all through the emphasis is on '*caveat emptor*' – let the buyer beware.

Statistics have it that most buyers become sellers on at least two occasions and frequently three. The first-time buyer tends to move after seven years to another property of higher value as his station in life has improved. Later he may move again, and generally at the end of his working days. That means he is at a given time both a seller and a buyer and in that case he wants a smooth transaction so that he is not left without a roof over his head or faced with hotel bills in an interim.

Selling through an estate agent

Selling a house can be simple or involved, depending upon the methods adopted. Estate agents are adept at selling; that is their main purpose in life. As in everything some are better at it than others so recommendation is an important aspect in deciding to whom the work should be given. Those with a good 'track record' of selling are obviously sound and efficient. It is a field in which names count as well as favourable comment and approval. There are benefits in using the services of an estate agent. Many expect a seller to pay for advertising costs above a certain figure; some insist that all costs for advertising are met by the seller. These and other questions should be cleared before any firm agreement is reached between an agent and seller. Bear in mind that the agent thus commissioned, acts for the client, the seller, not the purchaser. That being so he is charged with getting the best deal he can for the seller, which does not always mean the highest price offered but it usually does. The agent's driving force is to complete a sale as quickly as possible at as satisfactory a figure as possible. There is no gratification for either agent or seller in long delays.

Agents are open to criticism that they obtain large fees for very little effort in some cases. What efforts are made frequently depend very much upon the attitude of the seller, his client.

An agent is au fait with local situations, including prices at which certain styles of properties are likely to sell. Should a seller insist on putting too high a figure on his home, the chances of an early sale are greatly diminished. It is wise to take the advice of an agent on the question of price and to give him some leeway so that what is expected or something near it can be obtained. He will give advice after seeing the house and noting its condition and position. All this an agent does without charge and indeed there is no charge until a house is sold. Even if for some reason a seller withdraws a property from the market an agent is unlikely to levy a fee though he may ask for some contribution to advertising costs if these have been incurred. Thus on the basis of 'no sale, no fee' a seller may go ahead with confidence. He may make some stipulations. For example, he may wish to give his chosen agent a time limit for selling the property after which he may decide to ask another agent to seek a buyer if the first one has no prospective purchaser in hand.

This raises the question of whether or not to instruct more than one agent in the first place. The concensus of opinion is against that course. Obviously an agent who knows he has been given sole rights to sell will work (or should strive) harder to find a buyer. If agents know that others have the same house they are less inclined to bother, human nature being what it is. In any event, many agents undertake to cooperate so that if one has a particular type of property being sought by someone in another agent's office, they will normally get the two together.

Among advantages of using an agent is that he will prepare and circulate to interested parties particulars of a house being offered for sale. These particulars will give a broad outline of the property, usually with a photograph, so that intending buyers may have an idea of what is involved. Potential buyers are usually able to be taken over a property by an agent or his staff so that any questions arising can be answered. He is duty bound then to submit all offers made for the property to the seller who will decide whether or not one or any is acceptable. At that point the agent will hand over to the seller's solicitors for completion of the transaction. Most sellers using agents in fact do not use them to full advantage. When it has been decided that an agent should act in a sale, the vendor is best advised to leave everything from that point, to him. In other words, make him work for his fee, a situation he much prefers anyway. He should be provided with a key, given an indication when and when not it will be convenient for him to take prospective purchasers over the house and strict instructions about not allowing callers to discuss purchasing.

There are many people who have learnt the hard way, and to their cost, that it seldom pays to try and conduct sales oneself. Inevitably a buyer will make an offer – cash, he says – but when the time comes he is always a few hundred pounds short! It is difficult for a seller himself to investigate the financial status of a prospective buyer. An agent, being a third party is much better placed in this respect and he is also generally able to suggest or obtain additional financial help where necessary as most are agents for building societies and assurance companies too. Should a seller wish to handle a sale himself, a course to adopt is to advertise his house in newspapers and/or periodicals. Again, the choice can be difficult; certain houses are best advertised in certain media in a particular way. Some newspapers cater better than others for specific types of properties; magazines also tend to be noted for carrying certain categories of homes, and a great deal of money can be spent with little or no return unless a careful study is made of the market.

Using an estate agent or not is frequently a question of just how the property market is functioning at any given time. It has been quite plainly demonstrated in the past that, when house sales are booming, owners tend not to use the services of an agent; they feel, rightly or wrongly (often wrongly in fact) that they can do just as well without them and in any case can save his fees. As house sales become more difficult owners seek out agents again particularly if at the same time funds for mortgages are also more difficult to find. A result is that in both cases there are problems; during boom conditions agents have very few properties on their books thus the choice for buyers is considerably restricted. In times of more stringent economic circumstances agents have a surfeit of homes for sale without much competition for them, so that prices tend not to rise and, where quick sales are required, can actually drop. Broadly, trying to sell on one's own invariably means that there is a good amount of guesswork involved. Going back again to the boom of 1972/3 a period when house prices increased rapidly, they had been artificially held down by credit squeezes and when money became more easily obtained they rocketed up to where they would have been had there been no Government interference with credit. Many owners found it no problem to sell, but in most cases they settled for less than the market value at the time.

It might therefore be concluded that a danger of selling a house on one's own is that, at times of rising prices, a figure less than what could have been obtained will be accepted and in times of falling prices (should they happen as they did in 1974/5) a figure higher than can be expected will be demanded. Agents have a fair idea of what house price levels are at any given time and they can adjust asking figures up or down if necessary to fit in with ruling values. As agents are dealing with scores of properties they are able to gauge the degree of competition too, a situation which a self-seller can hardly know unless he is able to go round counting the saleboards (and that is not a reliable guide as in some districts agents have an agreement that saleboards will not be erected).

There is one way in which a seller can judge how the market is moving and that is to comb through the advertisements in the local paper to estimate what prices are expected for properties similar to that it is proposed to sell. If houses in other areas nearby are also studied the information can be useful when a further purchase is contemplated. Paying too much heed to gossip is fatal. Rumours that because Mrs Brown obtained £15,000 for her house yours must be worth another £2,000 or £3,000 is not a good guide to fixing an asking price! What Mrs Brown did obtain, and what she said she obtained, as well as what the neighbours allege she told them she got, do not necessarily add up to the same amount!

All told then, it is perhaps better to take some advice from someone

59

who is best placed to give it; an agent. He will certainly quote the figure you say you hope to sell for, but at the same time will indicate what he thinks is the true value under all existing conditions and it is fairer, less exhausting and quicker to listen to what he considers is the right price for the property concerned. If he takes on the house, bungalow, flat or maisonette he will expect to be paid a fee. This should be agreed with him before any action on his part. A good indication will be to count on paying him about two per cent of the selling price of the property when it is sold. If there is no sale, there is no fee. It is also to be clearly agreed just what his fee will cover. Generally, some if not all advertising costs are embraced as is the cost of inspecting the house and preparing sale particulars. The details of the property will be entered on a register, filed and made available to persons who are seeking that type of property in the price bracket into which it falls. The fee will almost certainly cover the cost of telephoning interested parties and of sending out copies of the particulars by post, as well as probably the inclusion of a photograph. A picture of the house may also be placed in the agent's window to attract passers-by. Advertising additional to the normal amount may have to be paid for but that should be covered in a separate agreement along with any other items which may be proposed.

Agents normally like a little room for manoeuvre too, so that the price of a property may be subject to offers based on the amount stated. That could be slightly higher than the figure actually expected, enabling buyer and seller to indulge in a little to-ing and fro-ing so that the seller ultimately obtains the price he had agreed to settle for and the buyer feels he has got something of a bargain!

In those periods, which occur at more frequent intervals than is usually supposed, when the market is patchy with little movement except perhaps in the categories in which the least expensive homes for a particular area are being offered, the agent is much more likely to find a purchaser than is an owner on his own. Again, because of his overall knowledge of the manner in which the market is reacting it is he who will in the final resort effect a satisfactory sale. That is generally because, though acting for the seller, an agent maintains a list of people wishing to buy – a service denied to an individual acting off his own bat. Additionally, his window displays are maintained so that even if a seller has a notice at his gate, the passer-by is not as likely to see it as if the details of the property were among those in an agent's office. Invariably too, an agent is able to tie in the cost of advertising a seller's house along with others he may be offering as part of his general tactics of alerting the public to his wares and services. A most satisfactory, if, in the eyes of some, completely defeatist way of looking at the whole business of selling is to accept the fact that nearly all those house-hunting visit estate agents, or, in Scotland, in addition the central premises now set up in many major towns and cities by solicitors engaged in house sales to peruse the lists of properties in the market.

There can be few more embarrassing situations than those in which a seller has to quiz potential buyers about their facilities for funding a purchase and to weed out the genuine from the capricious. Stories are told and repeated about couples who spend their weekends going the rounds of properties on the market, pretending they are interested parties. As it turns out they use their time to gain entry into other people's homes to see their style of living and to compare it with their own. Sometimes their visits are less harmless; they are spying out the land to estimate the vulnerability and worth of breaking in.

Agents come in for a share of criticism and there is no denying that some of them deserve it. Politicians, notably those to the Left, have tried often enough to usurp them and went as far some time ago to introduce for a trial period preparatory to permanence, estate agencies in a number of town halls. This was to have illustrated how unnecessary estate agents were. The experiment was a flop and the town hall nomads have generally packed their belongings and left. On the cards is a scheme for registering all estate agents and this is expected to come about in due course, though again it has been tried on several previous occasions, each time some Parliamentary quirk intervening to postpone or cancel the projected legislation.

For many years, and continuing, there has been public criticism, shared also by solicitors, that agents charge too much particularly since price increases have resulted in sending their fees, which are on a percentage basis, higher and higher. Scale fees, now abolished, were laid down some years ago by the professional bodies to which agents belong. They include the Royal Institution of Chartered Surveyors and the Incorporated Society of Valuers and Auctioneers. These bodies, along with the more recently-formed National Association of Estate Agents, regulate the profession, and the public, for its own sake, is well advised to look for the distinguishing letters ARICS or FRICS, ISVA and NAEA on a firm's title or after the names of the partners who run it. Apart from anything else, firms which are members or have partners who are members of these bodies submit to codes of conduct. They also have taken out insurance, bonding their members so that the public has redress should any of their number fall by the wayside owing moneys to people who have entrusted them with deposits as stakeholders.

There will always be the case of the seller who considers himself badly done by, though what the agents say about the public on occasion doesn't bear repeating either. Sellers might like to make up their own minds after reading a pamphlet published by the Incorporated Society of Valuers and Auctioneers called simply 'Selling a House'. While the document is a plea to use the 'professional' there are some basic principles worth noting, among them the acknowledged fact that anyone can sell his own house as there is no restriction on who can attempt the operation, just as there is no legal bar to do-it-yourself conveyancing. The point is – do you want to? Since November 1970 a Government order has prevented estate agents from mutually agreeing a scale of selling charges.

Commissions charged vary according to the type of property and the part of the country in which it is situated as certain agents have traditionally charged certain levels of commission independent of recommended scales of charges. As costs increase, so agents are having to pay out more to meet them. In 1980 some agents, particularly in London's West End, where overheads are high, were charging three per cent with the prospect of other rises. Even so, their charges are lower than those on the Continent where six per cent is general and has been for many years. According to the ISVA pamphlet a seller should never instruct a second agent to act while another still has sole agency. If a second agent introduced a purchaser the seller could find himself liable to pay commission to the sole agent as well as to the selling agent. Sole selling rights enable an agent who is so authorized, to charge a seller commission when the house is sold, whether he has introduced the purchaser or not. That being the case, sole selling rights should never be granted unless there is some compelling reason for doing so.

Selling by auction or tender

Among other methods of selling and buying are the private auction and the tender. In the former instance an auctioneer will generally select half a dozen or so likely buyers who will be invited to make bids, probably in sealed envelopes, with the proviso that they make a second offer should there not be an acceptable figure. Sometimes the private auction takes the form of asking the people interested simply to make bids against one another until one outbids the rest.

Tendering comes somewhere between private treaty sale and an auction. It is not used extensively but has become more common in recent years for certain types of property. Potential buyers are invited to tender under specific conditions. Normally individual tenders are not disclosed to other tenderers under any circumstances. Sellers reserve the right not to accept the highest or any tender. Agents handling sale by tender will disclose the conditions for tendering along with the particulars describing the property to be sold. A person desirous of buying the property will have to fill in and sign with his or her name and address, what is called the Form of Tender. He or she is then required to send or deliver the same, still attached to the particulars, along with a cheque in favour of the agent concerned in the disposal for a sum equal to ten per cent of the amount tendered, in a sealed envelope. The envelope will be required to be identified, marked 'Private and Confidential: Tender for . . .' and delivered to a stated address on or before a prescribed time on a particular date. Tenders must be for a definite sum. It is not customary for a tender for £ . . . above the next highest offer, or words to that effect, to be accepted as a genuine offer. On acceptance of a tender the ten per cent deposit is held by the agent as stakeholder. Unsuccessful tenderers have their cheques returned.

4

HOME OWNERSHIP IN RETIREMENT

The home-owner approaching retirement, given prudent saving, is in a much better position than his brother who is renting. A house which is paid for provides relatively inexpensive living for the days when pensions rather than salaries are the main consideration. In any event, it may be sold off to provide capital for alternative, smaller and less costly accommodation if that is desired. The capital which has built up in a property over many years often surprises even the most financially-conscious owner who frequently discovers that the value of his property is not only a healthy figure enabling him to swap it for a cottage, flat or bungalow but also to help along his general finances by giving him a balance to enable him to have something in the bank to spend on luxuries as against necessities, a very happy position in which to find oneself. An alternative for those less desirous of moving when they are elderly, living on a pension and faced with too costly outgoings for everyday living is to take out one of the agreements with organizations which will purchase the house but allow the owner and his or her spouse to live there during their lifetimes. Caution is advised however, and certainly an accountant or tax consultant should be brought in to give guidance on the advisability of taking such a step.

Where a pensioner is still paying tax at a high rate, the benefits of taking advantage of one of the schemes provided by a number of assurance companies and finance groups is worth looking at. Such institutions will make loans to the more elderly at up to 80 per cent of the value of their homes. The money raised by this method is used to buy one of the annuities which the various finance houses offer and the annuity is payable until the pensioner dies. At that point of course, the money goes back from the estate of the deceased. The amount of the annuity depends upon the age of the pensioner; in fact on his expectation of life. Thus a person aged 65 could expect to receive less than a person of 80. There are too, other factors, one being that interest will be charged on the loan, usually deductable before a company makes its annuity payment.

Simply, the key as to whether or not such a deal is worthwhile is the rate of tax payable by a pensioner and that is why it is often well worth paying a fee to have professional advice. Such professionals will also indicate which type of annuity and which company provides the best and most profitable scheme for the individual concerned.

Broadly, too, executors of a pensioner who has taken advantage of one of these schemes can obtain some relief from Capital Transfer Tax as they can exclude from the estate the loan which was used to purchase the annuity initially. Also taken into account by the companies is the fact that as prices for houses rise, thus increasing the value of a property on which an annuity is based, there can be further loans based on the new values of the properties concerned, with some proportionate rise in annuity payments – in fact keeping up with inflation and the cost of living to some extent at least. One salient point; a substantial amount of any annuity is tax-free, an incentive in itself these days. Despite the Equal Opportunities Commission and the Sex Discrimination Acts, women, whose lives actuarily are reckoned to be longer than men's, receive lower amounts. The irony of the whole thing of course is that, the younger a person is the less he gets a year (when he is likely to be most active and able to spend it) while at 80 or 90, annuities are providing substantial sums which possibly a person in that age bracket would have more difficulty in spending.

The key to it all really is how much tax liability an owner has. It is as a result a highly individual decision that has to be made. As an example, a widower of 75 taking a £10,000 loan on his house could effectively add more than £800 a year to his income.

Among organizations which either operate schemes or provide information on making an income from capital tied up in a house are Noble Lowndes & Partners, the Save and Prosper Group, Equitable Life Group, Unitholders Provident Assurance, Home Reversions, and City of Westminster Assurance Co., while the Home Owners Income Advisory Service exists to provide details of schemes best fitted for individuals according to their circumstances. Assistance to semi-retired and retired people in acquiring accommodation is also given by, among others, the Mutual Householders Association. The Association has been responsible for buying many large houses, some of them of period style and architecturally important, dividing them into self-contained flats and making them available for purchase. An advantage is often that owners who have hitherto maintained furniture considered too big for a modern house or flat can quite easily fit it into the generally more spacious rooms of these converted properties.

Owners of homes which have become much too large for their everyday needs might also try to find some relief in one of the several projects whereby an organization takes them over while allowing part of them for the occupants for their lifetime. Among the bodies which operate in this way is Help the Aged, which seeks properties suitable for converting to flats and maisonettes. The organization wants houses having from eight to 100 rooms as gifts for converting with the owner retaining a modernized self-contained flat or maisonette for the lifetime of himself and his wife, rent-free with allowances against rates and repairs. Such houses are sought in good neighbourhoods or centrally sited in towns, cities or villages. The charity has its own architects to handle such projects.

While there may be disadvantages in home ownership over the years there are advantages which far outweigh them. One and an important one is that it is an asset which always keeps pace with money values and it has been proved that bricks and mortar are not only the best but indeed, for most people, the only real hedge against inflation. At the end of a working life a house enables its owner to retire in at least some degree of the comfort he has built up and enjoyed during his younger days. At that time too, it is, as always, an asset which may be turned to to help in deciding future course of action.

Parts of large houses may be let if that is the inclination of the owners. Another way out is to take advantage of one of the schemes under which an organization will acquire the property for an agreed sum, allow an owner to live there (and his widow if that should arise) and then eventually take it over. This type of reversion is designed for retired people on fixed incomes who find the going harder each successive year as the cost of living rises. The attraction is that the home, the last thing most people wish to give up, is safeguarded for their lifetime, they were provided with an additional income while they continue to live in it and so are able to maintain their standards and enjoy the amenities they have worked for so long. One of the organizations specializing in this form of house transfer is Home Reversions.

Some building firms specializing in creating estates of retirement homes will buy an existing property owned by a potential purchaser of one of their new houses. There is not a list of such builders; indeed many adopt schemes such as this in periods when new properties are difficult to shift simply to get the market moving and to keep the money turning over at the bank!

A DICTIONARY OF TOPICS, TERMS AND PROBLEMS

LIST OF TOPICS IN PART TWO

A

Abstract of title The legal definition of details taken from title deeds. In the case of a property which does not have a registered title the abstract will, among other things, prove ownership of the seller.

Access from the highway Prospective home-owners require to know their rights of access to a highway. Most roads, depending upon their classifications are either the responsibility of local councils or the Government but there exist in certain areas private roads which residents maintain themselves under a collective responsibility. Where roads are maintained by the public authorities normal access to them is unhampered and a householder whose property fronts directly on to a road has no more rights over the thoroughfare than the rest of the community. Private roads, usually created in the past by estate developers, give on to main roads and it has become common practice for residents on such estates to request that the roads be taken over by the public highway authority concerned with the area.

Accountant It is well worth consulting a qualified accountant to find out the most advantageous method of house purchase. Advice of course must be on a personal basis as it is usually tied in with tax liability and other commitments and outgoings, including insurance. There are five main professional bodies looking after the interests of accountants and several smaller ones, Anyone can call himself an accountant so it is as well to choose a person who is a member of one of the more generally recognized organizations. These are the Institute of Chartered Accountants of England and Wales and its Scottish counterpart, the Association of Certified Accountants, the Institute of Public Finance and Accountancy. The latter two bodies are specialist organizations as their names imply.

Agreements In dealings with property everything should be recorded in writing. Verbal decisions should be confirmed by letter as soon as possible after they are reached and copies kept. Written agreements should be in plain, straightforward terms, setting out what has been decided upon and what has been agreed. Where money is concerned, the amounts involved should be stated. Agreements in this form do not only safeguard everyone's position but are invaluable should disputes arise or sadly, in the event of the death of one or other of the parties.

Special care should be taken to lay out clearly in writing discussions and decisions reached when on site with a builder or his workmen who are engaged say, to carry out alterations or extensions. It is easy to give orders for this or that to be done 'while the men are here' but such instructions can be costly and it is wise to satisfy oneself of what is involved by obtaining a written estimate of any new work which may be decided upon verbally as well as putting down just what was considered to have been agreed. Renovations can take much longer than is sometimes estimated or budgeted for and it is of use to everyone if there are clear and concise instructions, properly laid out and dated.

Air bricks Special bricks which are laid to allow ventilation in buildings. House-purchasers should always ensure that air bricks are performing their function and are not obstructed in any way, as lack of air can cause dry and wet rot. Air bricks and other ventilation traps such as metal grilles should always be inspected for stoppages and corrected if these are found.

Allotments Modern houses and flats have been built with little ground to spare for gardening. Sometimes it is possible to apply to the local council for an allotment. By law an allotment is a piece of ground not larger than 1,210 sq. yards and to provide allotments Parliament has passed several acts. Once allocated an allotment by a council (which retains powers to acquire land for the purpose of allotments) an occupier has security of tenure. In the past few years allotments have not always been taken up and some have been allowed to deteriorate until becoming sites for new home-building.

Ancient lights Not so ancient as the description implies, but a valuable safeguard for home-owners who might be faced with a new project which may deprive them of most of the light their properties enjoy. It is possible to lodge an objection to a development on the grounds of ancient lights where it is felt and can be proved that new building will interfere with light to an existing house. The law says an owner or tenant must have used the house or other property for at least 20 years before ancient lights can be substantiated.

Other obstacles which might interfere with an owner's enjoyment of his lights are also covered; for example a tree which has got out of hand and grown across a window blocking out the view completely, but in practice ancient light rights are difficult to establish.

Animals Those householders who keep pets should be aware of the law about them. Generally speaking, owners are liable for any damage or injury caused by dangerous animals, both domestic and wild. Only dogs are subject to licensing. Once a dog is six months old it must have a licence which is renewable each year for its lifetime. The law says they must be kept 'under control' which provides a wide range of offences where they are held not to be, from sheep-worrying to actual attacks on people. Normally cats are not held to be liable to their owners in the same way as dogs though there is no real distinction in law; it is only that cats cannot be controlled in quite the same way as their canine neighbours.

Anode To be found suspended in water tanks. Chemical reactions are set up in zinc tanks to which copper pipes are connected. To counteract this and the electrical currents which are created, plumbers frequently insert an anode in the zinc cold water supply tank in the roof space or top bedroom. The anode wears away itself; in fact it decomposes due to the interaction of the other chemicals and must be replaced to continue its work. An anode will last about three years on average and should be renewed just before it disintegrates. It may be easily inspected simply by pulling it up and looking at it. Well worth having one as it can save a great deal of trouble from corroded pipes and small leaks caused by electrolysis.

Apportionments The amounts which buyers and sellers are due to pay for outgoings such as rates when a house changes hands.

Architect A professional who is trained to transfer ideas for buildings into working drawings. He is commissioned by a developer, builder or private individual to prepare plans to scale so that these may be translated by workmen into houses and other buildings.

Architects are also in many cases planning consultants and have knowledge of town planning and building regulations. They frequently oversee projects to ensure that they are being constructed in accordance with the plans prepared. Some architects specialize in various branches of activity associated with development; thus there are landscape architects, others who are concerned mainly with interior designs, many who are commissioned as expert witnesses for public inquiries and so on.

Their principal professional body is the Royal Institute of British Architects, from whom those wishing to commission an architect may obtain the names of those practising within a certain area of the country, or indeed, anywhere, including those British architects who are employed overseas.

Architect-designed This is used to describe houses which an architect has designed to the buyer's own specifications and requirements. In order to build a house one must have a plot on which to build it and these can be difficult to find. Since the war land has been sold usually in large or fairly large parcels, mainly for acquisition by builders and developers who proceed to create estates.

Plots on such estates are invariably not for sale to individuals; only the houses subsequently built on them are offered. In a few instances, builders, and sometimes local authorities, have put in roads and services to small and select sites which are then offered. Prices of course, vary according to what is being made available and are based too, on the size and situation as well as on the general amenities around. On some coveted sea front stretches or perhaps in a particularly attractive setting in a woodland or by a river, a site for a single house can cost as much as

74

£20,000. It would be difficult, on the other hand, to discover anything worthwhile for less than £3,000 or £4,000.

In a number of instances, a plot would require the buyer to instal some form of service if main supplies were not available easily or already laid on to the immediate area. That in itself can be a costly and time-consuming operation, probably involving the installation of a septic tank, if mains drains are not laid to which a connection can be made, and that is a job for experts. Arranging for electricity for an individual isolated house can also be expensive, invariably very expensive, as many farmers have discovered. As for the buildings to go up on the plot, unless the owner is a handyman with friends who can help carry through the craftsmen's parts of the work, the cost of a competent builder can be prohibitive. Before committing oneself to a purchase of a plot, assurance should be sought that planning consent will be forthcoming or is already granted.

Planning permissions are the responsibility of the local authority in whose district the plot is situated. A call to the local office of the authority will suffice and the assistance of the planning officer and his assistants can be invaluable. They may give some hint about what type of building would be allowed, or perhaps more to the point, they will indicate what style would not!

In certain parts of the country there is insistence for example, that buildings should conform with those already existing; thus in many Yorkshire villages, new homes must be built in stone or its reconstituted equivalent as is also the case in the Cotswolds. Not only is stone one of the most expensive materials, but men skilled in stonework are few and so they too command top prices for their labour. Such general details may be invaluable in deciding whether or not it is a feasible project to buy a site to build one's own home on it.

There will also be the financial side to arrange; it is a good idea to discuss any project of this nature with a building society or insurance company. These institutions will lend on this type of development provided they are satisfied with the general scheme. The usual way is for them to provide finance at certain stages of building, so that as the work progresses there is money to meet the necessary outgoings for labour and materials.

Right at the start, the building society or other mortgagee will want to see and study plans of the proposed structure which your architect will have prepared. The architect will undertake also to obtain the necessary planning consent for the job as, even if there is an existing permission on the plot it will generally only be for 'consent in principle' and the local authority requires to pass plans which show in detail what is contemplated.

There will be a charge for the preparation of the plans and if desired the architect can also be commissioned to oversee the building work as it is carried out. From time to time officials of the local authority will also wish to inspect the job, ensuring that the work done complies with building regulations and by-laws. The regulations are there to ensure that work is completed to standards considered necessary and the local authority's surveyor is empowered to insist that they are met. It won't be long either, before a representative of the valuation department for the district pays a visit. The district valuer is soon off the mark in assessing a new place for rates!

As costs for new building tend to go up all the time; higher wages for workers, increased transport charges (which bear heavily if a plot being developed is at some distance from the supply centre), it is as well to account on a job landing the owner with considerably more outlay than at first anticipated. That is why it is essential to go into costings thoroughly at the start and to obtain estimates from more than one builder. Even then professional advice should be sought; the lowest tender is not necessarily the cheapest in the long run and a reliable, responsible firm with a sound record in the industry should be preferred to the company about which no one has had any experience.

Instead of employing an individual architect one can use one of several firms who operate a specialist service on the lines of the Worksop-based Rationalised Building Systems company, which has branches at Colchester, Essex and Barry, Glamorgan. These organizations will undertake to carry through a scheme in entirety; translate an idea on to paper, discuss the building style most applicable to the area and obtain planning consent.

They will supply all necessary drawings plus information about drainage, central heating circuits, kitchen layouts, sanitary fittings, fitted wardrobes and special exterior finishes where applicable. The foundations of a home are the responsibility of a site-owner and after that materials are delivered to the plot at proper intervals.

The basic plans and finishes can be varied; in fact with RBS systems there are some 2,000 variations of one sort or another, from special front doors to different coloured bricks. The RBS book of types gives 30 basic plans but the firm's service covers the whole sphere of building. As well as providing a full architectural service and back-up with materials, the company can assist right through all construction jobs from garages and garden stores to large estate projects, from a single farm bungalow to an adaptation of the company's designs for special uses and tastes.

There are some less costly alternatives to the individual architect-designed house. A number of builders owning substantial sites will build houses for buyers who are prepared to choose from one or other of several styles they proffer. An advantage of this course is that the builder will normally do the job for a fixed price, with the proviso that if there are variations they will be charged as extras. In this way a buyer is able to get a house which goes some way towards his ideal.

Area grants Local authorities designate 'Housing Action Areas' and/or

'General Improvement Areas'. The designation indicates the amounts of grants which may be made for improvements. In Housing Action Areas the limit is 75 per cent with up to 90 per cent in hardship cases; in General Improvement Areas 65 per cent; other areas 50 per cent. One grant, the Intermediate Grant, is available as a right; the others are discretionary. The Intermediate Grant is given providing the property when improved will reach a required basic standard and have a habitable life of at least 15 years. It is available to instal standard amenities, such as a fixed bath and so on. An Improvement Grant is intended for homes likely to be fit for habitation for at least 40 years while a Repair Grant is only avilable in Action or General Improvement Areas. It covers items not associated with other improvement work, and might for example include repairs to a faulty roof.

Assessment This is a valuation of a property, usually for rating purposes. On the assessment of a house the amount of rates to be paid by the occupier is worked out. The assessment is made by an inspector of the Inland Revenue who takes into consideration a number of factors, not least what it is estimated the property could be let for and also its situation in relation to other houses in the area, and their worth.

Assignment The procedure by which the leasehold interest in a property is conveyed to another.

Assurance policy While it is not necessary as a condition of obtaining a mortgage to take out a life assurance policy for the amount of the loan, it is usually recommended so that in the event of death, the borrowing is cleared off and dependants can continue to live in the property without meeting further mortgage repayments.

Other insurance should be taken out to cover the actual building and its contents. It is essential that the buyer covers the house he is buying as soon as contracts are signed, as he becomes liable once he has agreed to purchase.

Auctions These are public sales at which interested parties may go along and bid for what is being offered. Auctions may be the form of sale used for anything from houses, flats, shops, offices and factories to china and glass, furniture and bottles of wine. The sales are conducted under strict rules by an auctioneer, and goods are sold to the person making the highest bid for them. The auctioneer is always free to accept a bid or not and indicates the end of a sale by using his hammer to tap the table. It is customary for him to give plenty of time for a final bid to be made by making three well-spaced taps of the hammer before closing the sale.

Auctions take place on stated dates at stated times. They are advertised by auctioneers on posters and in newspapers and magazines. They indicate broadly what is to be sold and give the address of the property involved. Before the actual sale, a copy of the auctioneer's particulars of the property should be obtained. These may be sent through the post or can be picked up at his office. They give an outline of the property to be offered. In the particulars will also be printed what are called the Special Conditions of Sale, with the statement that what is being offered is being sold subject to those conditions with variations where they are appropriate to the specific property involved. These conditions are binding in law.

The conditions will give the name of the seller's solicitors and indicate when the sale will be completed, and where. Also included will be a description of the property's tenure – freehold, or leasehold – and will indicate previous as well as the present owners. Also indicated will be disclaimers, if any, about such things as restrictions which might exist under the Town and Country Planning Acts, wayleaves, rights of way for drainage and so on, charges and fees, and any other documents which may have had a bearing on the sale.

It is essential that a buyer, before embarking on a bidding spree, should be fully aware of the implications of the Conditions of Sale and his solicitor is the best person to peruse them and to advise whether or not there are snags which may impede the purchaser in pursuit of his goal.

An accepted bid presupposes that a contract has been entered into for the property or other goods offered. In the case of sale of property, a bidder will be required to sign a contract on the spot and lodge ten per cent of the purchase price as a deposit. The contract will also stipulate the date of completion for the sale when the balance of the purchase money will be required.

Before attending an auction a prospective buyer should make absolutely certain what the property in mind is worth, and a professional valuation is a wise first step. A second, is to make the necessary financial arrangements to enable a purchase to be completed.

A building surveyor should be asked to inspect the property concerned for defects, and, if requested, give an indication of its value. For these services a fee should be agreed before asking the surveyor to do the work. If a prospective purchaser is so inclined, the surveyor or an estate agent will go along to the auction and bid on his behalf.

Sometimes this is the advisable course to take as, in the heat of the chase in an auction room, some people can be carried away by the thrills of competition and bid far more than they intend to, or indeed can afford. A bid, once made, is binding.

Only strong personalities therefore, should take on the task of making bids! These incidentally, may be made in any form recognizable to the auctioneer as genuine. A flick of the auction particulars or any piece of paper, a nod, broad wink, upturn of the eyebrows, a wave of the finger, all are known to the astute man on the rostrum and he watches for any and every sign.

By the time the auction is held, everything should be clear in the mind of the prospective buyer, though at the actual event, before asking for bids, the auctioneer will endeavour to answer any questions which may have cropped up or been raised since the particulars were printed.

Occasionally what is known as a disclosed reserve price will be given. That is the figure below which the property concerned will not be sold and in fact may be interpreted as an invitation to those interested to make their bids from that point. Generally however, a reserve will not be disclosed and the auctioneer will start the sale by asking what he is bid for the property, for someone to 'start him off', or he may suggest 'Who will give me £x?'. From there bidding proceeds with the auctioneer indicating the amounts being represented by each bid. For instance, in the case of a house bids may go up in £1,000s, then £500s, then £100s, possibly £50s and £5s. Somewhere in the sale the auctioneer may give a hint by saying 'I'm going to sell this property', which means that bidding has reached the level at which the seller is willing to sell. What the property fetches above that is what the final bidder is prepared to pay for it. At the end of the sale, the successful bidder will be required there and then personally or through his representative to sign a contract and pay ten per cent of the full purchase price, that is, the price which he has just agreed by his bid to pay.

What is called a Memorandum of Contract is printed on the back of the auction particulars, with spaces provided for the name and address of the purchaser. This memorandum acknowledges that the buyer has bought the property described in the particulars for the sum of £ . . . and has paid to the auctioneers, as stakeholders, £ . . . (representing ten per cent or more) as a deposit and in part payment of the purchase money. In the memorandum, the buyer also agrees to pay the remainder of the purchase money and to complete the purchase in accordance with the already referred to Special Conditions. The memorandum is witnessed, the purchase price, deposit and balance due being set out, and the memorandum is then signed by the auctioneers as agents for the seller, confirming the sale and acknowledging, as stakeholder, the deposit paid. Details are then sent to the buyer's solicitor, whose name is also filled in on the memorandum. The names of the seller's solicitors are always included on the front of the particulars.

By this method the two solicitors then get in touch and arrange contracts and completion dates. If a mortgage is required to complete the sale, arrangements for this will have been made by the purchaser prior to his bidding for the property and he will also have seen his bank manager if a bridging loan of some sort is necessary while the legal formalities are gone through. Often completion is synchronized so that a seller of a property who is also buying another can move with a minimum of inconvenience and solicitors are adept at juggling things so that a number of buyers and sellers all complete their transactions within a few days of each other.

Authority to inspect The documents despatched to the Land Registry by or on behalf of an owner to another person, usually a purchaser's solicitor, by which the latter obtains authority to extract details from the register of a property.

B

Beetles Small areas of the South-East are particularly prone to the attention of the House Longhorn beetle which attacks softwood timbers. The Building Research Establishment undertakes surveys from time to time and since the 1950s as a result areas considered to be at risk from the beetle have been subject to building regulations specifying that all sofwoods used in the construction of roofs must be pre-treated to prevent infestation.

Most infestations have been found to be within the area bounded by Bracknell, Leatherhead, Haslemere and Basingstoke and the worst districts for infestation are stated to be Camberley, Walton-on-Thames, Weybridge and Horsham. There is some indication of a slight spread to the north-east of the principal area and some in a sector south of London while infestation has also been reported from the South Coast. Along with roof timbers the insects have penetrated other joinery as well as doors and floors. The Building Research Establishment is always ready to dissect information relating to beetles so that up-to-date mapping can be undertaken.

Bills Sellers should ensure that all bills are paid up to the date when they leave a property. Gas and electricity services will read meters for that purpose. Rates are usually paid either half-yearly or quarterly and the easiest way if they have been paid already is for the buyer and seller of a house to apportion their shares. Normally the seller meets the rates up to the date on which he vacates and the buyer takes on the charge on the day he goes into the house. If the seller has paid rates past the date on which he leaves he can claim a rebate. Some local authorities levy rates or a proportion of them on vacant property and where that is the case the date of completion is the date at which the rates responsibility changes from seller to purchaser.

Borrower One who obtains funds in the form of a loan, usually a mortgage, to buy a home. The commonest borrowing is that done from the building society but other ways of obtaining financial assistance in purchasing include those from local authorities and life assurance companies, as well as from a bank or a private source. Some finance companies will also advance funds for house purchase and some firms provide assistance to employees, often at advantageous rates of interest.

Boundaries These should be clearly known. Nothing is liable to cause more dispute and bad feeling than encroachment by one person on another's property, so boundaries should be known and respected. Normally house deeds and plans show boundaries and these are marked by posts or fences or both. It is often desirable to know exactly where a boundary runs as a few inches may make the difference between being able to do some improvement or not. For example, if it is proposed to extend a house or build a garage, six or seven inches one way or another may be vital. On modern estates boundaries are sometimes obscure where front drives are common to a pair of houses and there are rules as well as good neighbour relations regarding shared drives (q.v.).

Bridging loan An advance made to provide financial help while a person purchasing one house is in the process of selling another.

Builder A person or firm carrying on building operations. Reputation is a great asset in this branch of activity as many so-called builders are little more than jobbing tradesmen and some leave much to be desired in that direction too. Choosing a builder to complete a job depends very much upon the type of work required. There are usually local people who can and will recommend one or another builder depending upon what is proposed to be done. Local authority surveyors and estate agents also are able to help and the National Federation of Building Trades Employers carry lists of member-firms, as does the National House-Building Council (q.v.). In many towns and regional centres, there are local associations of builders whose members can be recommended to execute various forms of work. The building trade itself is divided into several specialist groups which deal with certain aspects of building such as roofing, plumbing, electrical work and so on. Usually a builder or building firm will have its particular specialist contractors on which to call.

Building centre Manufacturers and suppliers of building and associated materials have a show area in London where the latest products are displayed to public view. The centre embraces an advisory service and technological section. Anyone interested in inspecting the latest styles, colours and applications of any building materials (within reason) will find them at the Building Centre or there will be someone on hand to indicate where it is possible to see them. At the same time, manufacturers of certain products also have display showrooms of their own, for example, the ceramic firms. The Building Centre will give details of almost everything connected with building and it is an ideal place into which to wander when a new or redesigned home or an extension is planned.

Building Research Establishment The research body for the building industry with its laboratories in Aylesbury. Undertakes a wide range of inquiry and produces reports on materials and methods; issues recommendations which are, if necessary, introduced into building regulations by the Government and local authorities. The organization also operates an advisory service from its research station.

Building societies These are organizations which provide funds for those wishing assistance in buying their own homes. The funds are made available by moneys deposited with them which attract interest for those investing.

The building society movement started in a small way as a type of self-help where people with money to invest did so with the prime object of building up a central fund from which they could in due course borrow to buy their own homes. Some societies have become national concerns with branch offices in major towns and cities throughout the British Isles; others have maintained a purely local role.

Estimates indicate that there are more than 40 societies, most of which are members of the Building Societies' Association, the body which recommends rates of interest to be paid to investors and borrowers from time to time as circumstances alter. Societies are not bound to accept the levels of rates of interest proposed by the Association though the majority does. Sometimes the smaller societies charge interest rates slightly above the Association's recommended rates and these also have special rates for borrowing on property which is not to be exclusively occupied by the person borrowing.

Buying Purchase of a home should be undertaken whenever it is felt the time is ripe. The time is ripe in fact when a person knows exactly what he wants and has taken the correct advice on how best to arrange to pay for it. House prices should not in general be taken as an indication of when to buy. When to buy is whenever the financial ability to do so is attained. A precaution should be to have saved consistently with a building society or to have taken out an insurance policy specifically earmarked for future house purchase.

Buyers will require to put down a certain amount of the purchase price as an initial deposit and it is wise to count on having not less than ten per cent of the price of a property it is intended to buy.

Buying involves a strictly laid-down set of legalities and while it is possible to carry out these individually most buyers use and are advised to use a solicitor. It is also usually sensible practice to obtain an independent survey and valuation of any property it is proposed to acquire. The rule is 'let the buyer beware' and faults later discovered cannot easily be rectified.

The following is a list of steps which should be taken when buying a home. 1 count up funds and decide what can be afforded. 2 choose the district in which it is proposed or desired to live. 3 match up the price of the house with the actual or hoped-for funds, at the same time having quizzed a building society, preferably one in which an investment or some savings have been lodged about the mortgage advance if one is desired. 4 find the house or flat which fits most nearly what is wanted and in the price range which fits the pocket. 5 inspect the property, make certain it is near what is wanted, even if it falls short in some directions. 6 obtain an independent valuation and, on that basis, make an offer, pay a holding deposit. (If the property is new there may still be some room for bargaining.) Meantime, lodge an application for a mortgage if required and instruct a solicitor to act on the legal side unless a 'do-it-yourself' operation is decided upon. 7 time for contracts to be prepared in draft form if offer is accepted. At this stage the solicitor or self-operating buyer will undertake to make the necessary inquiries about the title and local searches to iron out or see there are no snags or impediments to sealing the deal. 8 approval of draft contract and, hopefully, an offer of a mortgage of the size requested. 9 exchange of contracts between buyer and seller with relevant documents concerning the mortgage and any balance of moneys due to date. 10 completion of purchase. 11 paying the bills for conveyancing, and so on, with added VAT on solicitor's account.

C

Capital Gains Tax This is the tax paid on the profit realized when an asset, such as a house and property, is disposed of, but it is not levied in cases where the property being sold is the main residence of the owner and the exemption applies to an acre of garden or more if the area involved is necessary for the 'normal enjoyment' of the house. On a second home, Capital Gains Tax is applicable, but as it implies, the tax is only on the gain, that is, the profit made in a transaction and not on the full amount involved in the deal.

Even when Capital Gains Tax is applicable most of those eligible to pay it will find they have an option. They can elect to be charged at full income tax rates on one half of the gain up to £5,000.

The tax is levied after expenses have been allowed and an owner is given the right, when two houses are involved, to choose which is his main residence to be exempt from the tax. Places which are let to tenants do not qualify as the houses must both be residences in the true sense of the word, of the owner.

A new relief was included in the 1980 Budget, which allows the first £10,000 of gains on that part of your house which is let separately, up to and in addition to the amount of the gain on the portion occupied by the owner, to be tax free too.

Where a property has been a person's only or main residence for part of the period of ownership, special considerations are given. Three years' absence can be claimed for whatever the reason and a further four years because of a change of job with in addition any time spent working abroad. A stipulation is that a person must have lived in the house both before and after the periods of absence and that there is no other house which could rank for exemption. In such cases Capital Gains Tax would be worked out on a part-liability and part-exempt basis.

Houses which are used exclusively for a business are subject to the tax but a room used partly for business and partly as a normal room in the house will not normally be liable to the tax.

Anyone liable for Capital Gains Tax on a house can get some idea of the amount to be paid by subtracting from the proceeds of the sale the actual costs of selling. These cover items such as estate agents commission, solicitors' fees, any necessary advertising and so on. Capital Gains Tax is then levied at the current rate on the balance.

Cavity wall Most modern homes have cavity walls formed by building an outside skin with facing bricks and an interior of either a rougher brick or breeze block. They are kept apart by a cavity of two inches and are bound at intervals by metal ties. Recent methods of insulation to retain heat pour or pump in special materials to fill the cavity. The alternative is a solid wall cement rendered with a waterproofing agent.

Central heating Since the last war, central heating has become the popular way to ensure that a home is comfortably warm. There are various forms of central heating, depending upon the fuel used. The choice broadly is between oil, gas, electricity and solid fuel. Modern central heating installations use thermostats to control the levels of temperature both at the point of fuelling and in individual rooms. While the tendency has been for recently-built homes to have central heating installed as part of the building, older homes can easily be given the treatment.

Costs are governed by the type of installation and the number of rooms it is proposed to heat. Radiators and hot-air systems are most commonly used. There are 'do-it-yourself' kits and exponents, but it is a job for a specialist really. Area gas and electricity boards have recommended contractors to do the work and some boards also have their own contracting departments. Central heating, to be effective, requires arithmetical computations which are worked out by a specialist in the field.

Not every house responds most effectively to the same type of central heating and it is wise to investigate the running costs of the different systems before committing oneself. Emphasis is on fuel saving and efficiency which presupposes proper insulation so that there is no unnecessary wastage.

Two types used are water and hot air. In the first water is heated and circulated via pipes and radiators or convectors, in the second, air is warmed and blown out into rooms through ducts. Electricity, gas, oil or solid fuel can be used in either type. There are variations on the themes and from time to time, due to changes in costs, one form of fuel is more advantageous than another.

It is however, generally assumed that gas central heating is as good value for money as can be obtained and that electric under-floor or storage heating is the least profitable except to the electricity boards! With the drive for smokeless zones, coal which produces fumes and dirt, is gradually receding in popularity, though there are smokeless grades which are efficient and cost certainly no more than gas. Oil seems to be subject to the vagaries of the Arab oil sheikhs and the progress of North Sea operations.

Progress is being made with solar heating, a form which requires little outlay but which involves problems over storage. These will doubtless be solved in due course and meanwhile there are homes where solar heating installations provide ancillary sources quite successfully and very inexpensively. Apparently even in areas where sunshine is a scarce commodity in the winter months there is a sufficient supply of its essential rays to ensure that this type of heating system is well beyond the purely experimental stage as a major source for the household.

Cesspool In earlier days, many houses were not served by main drainage and sewage disposal for the household was into a deep hole known as a cesspool. Liquids seeped away naturally but solids had to be removed from time to time. Some of the older houses in remote country areas still have cesspools though these days they are more likely to have either a chemical closet or a septic tank.

Character property Estate agents like to call the individually-styled property one of 'character' if that description fits. Ask what it means and there is no definable answer. Many prewar, well-built and nicely-sited among the larger houses however, do, for want of a better word, fall into the category of having 'character' and possibly the best way of describing it is that they look solid and comfortable with an air of slight superiority. Anyway, they sell well and appeal to those who seek something less modern than new and more modern than period, in which these days one would include early-Victorian which in any case was often a copy of late-Georgian.

Houses of 'character' have been somewhat lacking since the last war when the emphasis has been on complying with planners' demands which mainly appear to have been to cram in as many homes as possible on a particular site – hardly a recipe for 'character' building. Perhaps the nearest to it have been the attempts at 'cluster' housing, which again is not everyone's hod of bricks. Thus a house having that indefinable something is usually one built just at the turn of the century or up to 1914, or again in the 1920s when some particularly fine specimens were raised. The best of these houses now sell at figures which would make their first owners and builders gasp with amazement.

Many of them followed no particular design or pattern and were frequently built to specific demands for individuals. Others, including some built in recent years, are unashamedly copies of Georgian styles and there are mock-Elizabethan and mock-Tudor buildings which continue to fall into the category. Several of the latter, might it be said, most firmly do not! The connoisseur will seek the genuine article among the country's store of period properties.

Today Victorian and Edwardian semi-detached houses, frequently restricted to three or four bedrooms are as likely as not to sell as quickly as any other style though their lofty elevations mean they are costly to maintain and renovate.

In Edwardian days and up to the end of the 1920s, houses were spacious without being clumsy as is often the case with Victorian building and builders in the days before the advent of the estate three-bedroom semi-detached in 1930 produced some of the best of modern housing. These included handsome four- to seven-bedroom homes with fine joinery, frequently oak for floors, doors and panelling, which today are invariably described as being 'properties of character'

Charge certificate The Land Registry certificate provided for a mortgagee of a property having a registered title.

Charge Register A section of the register at the Land Registry which shows details of mortgages, covenants and other interests which might apply to the person registered as owner of a property.

Chartered Surveyor Qualified surveyor who is a member of the Royal Institution of Chartered Surveyors (ARICS or FRICS). He can be a specialist in a number of branches; quantity surveying (preparing bills of quantities for building and civil engineering jobs); building surveying (trained to inspect and report on the state of new and existing buildings); land surveying, usually engaged on extensive land projects in agriculture or civil engineering); general practice surveying (house sales and related subjects).

Chief rent A payment made by the owner of a freehold property similar to a ground rent paid by a leaseholder to a ground landlord. A chief rent is usually a small sum due yearly and can now be acquired by the freeholder. Chief rents were most common in the Manchester area and other parts of Lancashire where builders retained an interest in the land on which they had erected homes so obtaining an income from it.

Choosing a house Basically the only way to choose a house is first to choose the district in which it is proposed to live. Most people are restricted, due to employment, to a limited area and it is pointless to trek hither and thither looking at houses which are too distant to make sense. Some people have skills, or money (or both) which enable them to live wherever they wish. In those circumstances it is possible to choose simply the house itself rather than a house in a particular locality. All manner of other considerations arise, of course; it is little use choosing a house where there are no schools if it is hoped to educate a family at a day school; properties in remote spots are difficult if a wife is left on her own all day without transport.

Clean air legislation Since 1968 the Clean Air Act has governed the amount of smoke and fumes which factories may emit and chimneys must be sufficiently tall so as to prevent fumes being a health hazard to people in the vicinity. Householders are affected too, by smoke control orders in force in various parts of the country under which it is an offence to emit smoke from fires. Smokeless zones are well defined and local authorities will demonstrate where the boundaries are. It is policy to make the whole country a smokeless zone in due course, but this will take time. In smokeless zones it is necessary to use special solid fuels where these are applicable. They are more expensive than ordinary house coal. House-buyers should always investigate whether or not a property they wish to purchase stands in a smokeless zone.

Coastal homes Naturally, many couples, after years of being cooped up in landlocked situations turn their attention seawards when they change their job or retire. Their choice lies between the lusty breeziness of the North-East coasts and the calmer, softer climate of the Cornish Riviera. The variety from one extreme to the other is huge, and the weather, if that is the key factor, is unpredictable everywhere. At the coast the sun when it shines can be extremely hot or shrouded in mist, the winds when they blow can be stronger and the ground better or worse for certain plants and flowers.

There has been much change in seaside resorts since the last war, both in visual terms and in outlook. Many have altered considerably, becoming instead of seaside towns, towns which happen to be on the sea. Gone are the days when they catered for the holidaying families for a fortnight; even the most popular of them these days find the day tripper in the ascendancy. A result has been the demise of many hotels or their conversion to flats.

With more attention being paid too, to encouraging industry to establish itself and to provide work for younger people, the age groups have become more evenly balanced, whereas previously there was a markedly higher proportion of elderly.

Changing emphasis however, has also provided more competition for homes which used to be acquired by retired couples. Large estates of bungalows which were developed with the eyes on the retired purchaser, now accommodate many young people, some with families, who have found employment locally. The competition has increased prices for bungalows. At the same time, many resorts have only allowed small family homes in terrace or semi-detached styles where once bungalows would have been built. Flats and maisonettes have also superseded bungalows in many areas.

With a greater variety in houses, prices have tended not only to stabilize, but to nudge closer together irrespective of area. The gap of

£3,000 to £5,000 which a seller in the London area or from Birmingham could have counted on between what he obtained for his home against what he would have to pay say in Devon or Cornwall, has largely disappeared.

The increased popularity of water sports, notably sailing, has correspondingly increased pressure on seaside accommodation, and therefore on prices. Yachtsmen seeking a pied-à-terre have been strong competitors for houses, flats and cottages right on the waterfronts close to harbours and marinas. Least expensive homes at the coast are obviously those where competing factors are fewest so that money can be saved by looking around.

Proximity to the water adds to the price so just how far a person is prepared to be from the water dictates to some extent what he will have to pay. In large resorts such as Bournemouth, a buyer can be six miles from the sea so that prices in the backland area are no more than elsewhere. For windy headlands there are former costguard cottages on remote points which contrast with the fronts of South Coast towns like Brighton, Eastbourne and Worthing, all these days, to an extent commuter districts for London, just as in Yorkshire, Scarborough and Filey have some pressures from the West Riding towns. Buyers however, can pay dearly, literally, for views from waterside flats and penthouses as indeed is the case in such retirement haunts as Torquay and Sidmouth, Folkestone and Hastings, Newquay and Plymouth, all of which have today some element of employment alternative to the tourist trade. It is quite possible for a seafront flat to be up to £5,000 dearer than its counterpart a few streets behind.

A point to observe where limited incomes are operating is that the weather can play havoc with decorations at the seaside. Salt air goes for paintwork, but there are external yacht varnishes which are suitable for outside jobs and which are more resistant than ordinary paints. Window frames are specially susceptible to salt and buyers should check them carefully for deterioration, particularly if they are metal.

Watch the leaning trees to learn how hard the prevailing winds blow, and study the state of the gardens. Homes which are very exposed to the elements must inevitably be considered more vulnerable and therefore more costly to maintain than those in sheltered situations.

Low-lying properties can be in danger from flooding notably where winds have a reputation for being more than just a disagreeable nuisance. In the North-East and East coastal towns, winds can whip up high seas while across the country, say at North-West resorts like St Annes, Morecambe and Southport, the atmosphere can be surprisingly calm and temperatures on the whole less vicious.

Raging seas and dramatic scenery and weather are provided along the Atlantic coast of Cornwall where the climate contrasts greatly with that along the south coast of the same county. Prices tend to reflect the situation by being easier on the Atlantic side.

Warmed by the Gulf Stream, the West coast of Scotland can be surprisingly mild despite its Atlantic connections and there are places where palm trees grow quite happily out of doors. In parts of the Lake District, too, though wetter, semi-tropical plants are tempted to thrive. Close to the lakes themselves, however, prices again surge upwards as there are so few homes to be had in the area, and no new building is allowed.

Completion The point at which the necessary documents are handed over in return for the price paid for a property. Most contracts stipulate a date when completion must take place.

Completion statement This sets out what a buyer should pay at completion or a transfer of a property. It is prepared by the seller or his representative and shows the price, the deposit lodged and what proportions of other outstanding charges should be paid.

Compulsory purchase Local and national authorities have wide powers of compulsory purchase. One of the purposes of pre-sale searches is to ensure that a house or flat is not subject to, nor likely to be subject to, as far as one can ascertain, compulsory purchase. As well as the Government and the local councils, other public bodies are also empowered under certain circumstances to buy a property compulsorily. The land on which a house stands may be considered to be 'in the way' of a large-scale public authority development project or is needed for widening a road or creating a trunk road, ring road or motorway.

There is provision for anyone faced with the compulsory acquisition of his home to object but it is normally wise to obtain legal assistance. Where a compulsory purchase is won, the owner is entitled to compensation for his property at a figure based on what it would have fetched in the open market in a free and unfettered sale. There can also be additional payments for disturbance and for any other loss which can be proved as a result of the owner losing his home. Sometimes a local authority will consider itself morally committed to rehousing a dispossessed owner. Often, where several properties are involved, a public inquiry will be held at which objectors can put their case.

Condensation Inadequate heating and ventilation cause condensation which progressively can mean that mould eventually grows on walls. There is a new British Standard (BS 5250) on the control on condensation in homes, which sets out three basic design requirements to prevent it; warmth, reasonable ventilation and the use of materials which themselves are capable of being warmed rapidly by the inclusion of thermal insulants.

Most houses having cavity wall construction respond to the remedy of having the cavity filled with a dry insulating material such as Rockwool. This material stops water percolating across it. The system is Scandinavian and Rentokil has the sole UK rights. The company says it can be used anywhere in Britain so long as the walls are basically sound.

The Rentokil service has on official *agrément* certificate and is accepted by local authorities. It carries a 30 year guarantee. There is an information and advice service from the company's offices.

In new houses condensation is the most common problem next to shrinkage. Sometimes owners, concerned about dampness which they consider might be due to some structural defect, discover that condensation is the real culprit. Condensation is the moisture produced when warm damp air, vapour or steam comes into contact with any cold surface – windows, walls, and floors. A Department of the Environment leaflet on the subject says it can damage clothes, bedding, floor covering, decorations and the house itself. Condensation can spread from one room to another. Moisture from cooking, bathing, washing and drying clothes as well as from paraffin heaters and flueless gas heaters, even breathing, produces condensation. Keeping a window open and a door closed when it is 'steamy' is a sound way to combat the danger. In cold weather some heating should be maintained at all times.

Conditions of sale Terms which are contained in a contract signed between a seller and buyer of a property. They are one of three styles, National, those prepared by the Law Society and what are known as Statutory Conditions of Sale.

Contents insurance Home-owners are warned against allowing the amount for which the contents of their properties are insured to fall below their replaceable value. It is very easy in inflationary times to disregard the fact that should some misfortune strike and the contents of a home be destroyed the money for which they are insured is inadequate. A wise course to adopt is to take out a policy with an assurance company which automatically links the amount insured with the rising cost-of-living index thus keeping pace with things automatically. At the same time it should be checked that the insurance cover is for replacements at current prices, not at prices reigning at the time of purchase. Remember the £20 carpet will be closer to £500!

Contract The agreement, a legally-binding document which is really in two parts, one for the seller and the other for the buyer and which each signs. The signing is followed by the exchange of contracts, that is the two parts are swapped which then commit both the seller to sell to the purchaser and the purchaser to complete the deal.

The contract will contain what are termed Special Conditions of Sale, which among other things, could include a list of items which are not fixtures but which may be sold along with a house. Where the whole premises were being sold fully furnished the conditions of sale would say so. It may on the other hand specify that chattels, fittings and separate items specified in an inventory attached, are included for a certain sum.

Apart from permanent fixtures there are often other pieces of equipment which sellers are prepared to leave on a nominal payment. These frequently embrace such items as curtain rails and tracks designed to fit a special shape, say a bay window, bookshelves and mirrors, appliances which have been built-in or plumbed-in but which could be removed easily if necessary. Fitted cupboards and furniture specifically made for a house are permanent fixtures and must be left.

Contractor A firm, often a specialist in its field, which undertakes work for another. In building and developing, subcontracting is common as there are specialist operators for almost every sector of the construction industry. Many of the firms also are members of a trade organization which will provide names for those interested in using their services.

Conversions These usually involve turning a derelict property into a comfortable modern home. It is a mistake to embark on any major house conversions without going fully into the pros and cons. There must be full understanding of planning procedures and other regulations and all they embody. Some useful information on all aspects of the rehabilitation of residential property is contained in a leaflet issued by the Royal Institution of Chartered Surveyors in which guidance is given about using the professional services of a building surveyor.

In the leaflet an outline of procedure includes initial survey, feasibility, design, choice of contractor, legislation, contract, supervision, and so on. It says that a detailed structural survey will provide information about the condition of the property and its potential, together with a guide as to the costs which may be involved. In many cases there can be an extension of the structural survey to provide specific advice on the potential conversion and improvement of a property including sketches and budget figures of the costs and the best possible use of available space. Where appropriate there would be consultation with the local authority and other interested bodies. In the event of a decision being made that the property is capable of rehabilitation, the building surveyor will prepare detailed drawings and a written specification describing the materials and workmanship required for the proper execution of the work. Treatment for rising dampness and timber defects is only part of the wide specialist knowledge which may be required.

Guidance can also be given on the best forms of heating and insulation. This is not only important to the enjoyment of the property but also to the national need to conserve fuel.

The building surveyor will also, if asked, suggest the type of contractor most suitable for the job and any specialist companies which should be employed. He will obtain estimates on behalf of his client, and, as building regulations and government legislation affecting property are seldom static, he will keep up to date through official publications and daily contacts, liaising with the appropriate departments of local authorities. Thus he is well-qualified to submit formal applications covering plans, building regulations, fire precautions and other statutory requirements.

There are standard forms of contract drawn up by the Joint Contracts Tribunal. These are designed to protect both client and contractor. A building surveyor will advise on the suitable form of contract for the project in hand, will be available for a contractor to consult on unforeseeable snags and will hold regular site meetings during the progress of the work.

The RICS points out that when a building surveyor is not employed, occasionally relations between a client and builder become 'very strained' at the final stage of the project. A building surveyor will ensure that cost control has been properly exercised throughout the contract, so that the parties know in advance the approximate final cost.

Another method is to choose a house or bungalow from a book of plans. Such books contain scores of different house types from which to select and from which working drawings can be extracted for the planning authority and builder. What might be termed a halfway house can be evolved from a building already in existence occupying a site which attracts. The building might be anything from a derelict cottage to a former chapel, perhaps an outmoded school or mill, maybe what was once a coastguard's lookout or indeed a disused farm block, a stable perhaps, or a barn, or an oast-house.

Conversions of buildings of these types can be rewarding, but unless they are expertly carried out they rarely satisfy. Someone with a real flare for such jobs is needed to put a propsective owner on the correct track and the work of conversion too, is a task for the experienced craftsman and so is seldom cheap.

Most local authorities are only too happy to consent to the rehabilitation of derelict, near-derelict and unwanted buildings which have served their usefulness for the purpose for which they were originally provided. Most authorities will withdraw orders they have issued for closing such buildings or for their demolition if an acceptable scheme for converting them is drawn up.

As far as the buyer of the buildings is concerned, he frequently finds that they provide him with a site for a home which otherwise would not be available as it is within an area designated as a green belt or perhaps as one of particular beauty in which consent for new building is not given.

In the case of former mills, it has been possible for an owner of that type of building to provide himself with a waterside home in surroundings which almost certainly he would not have achieved any other way. The same is true of wayside chapels and small churches near hamlets in the Dales from which are unrestricted views over miles and miles of moorlands.

Just as for a new home, planning permissions are necessary for all major conversions as they are for a number of relatively minor ones.

Most conversions involve some extensions to the existing structure as well as the installation of amenities like a hot water system and bathroom. It is sometimes the case where there is a protection order on the exterior of a particular building – this can happen if it is a special example of the type of construction of its period – that a whole new home is built inside the exterior 'shell'.

Depending upon the building to be converted and the end product, it may be possible to obtain a grant to meet the cost of some of the improvements. Local councils make the grants and will also often provide a loan, though in times of economic stringency these are harder to get and not so generous as on other happier and more flush occasions. Grants are made on houses built before 1961 to provide homes with what are called standard amenities. These are a hot and cold water supply, a fixed bath or shower, washbasin, sink and inside w.c. It is emphasized, and will be re-emphasized by councils, that these standard amenities will be paid for on the basis of adequacy and not luxury. Above the standard grants are discretionary grants, designed to update old houses, to enlarge small ones and to convert former non-residential buildings. Owners of large properties who wish to divide them into flats are also eligible.

Conveyance The legal document, the title deed, which conveys ownership from one person to another in the case of an unregistered property. A registered property is conveyed to another party by a transfer and a leasehold by an assignment of the deed.

Conveyancing The legal work associated with conveying the ownership of a property from one party to another. It is used in connection with an unregistered property and the document, known as the title deed, contains details of the rights and interests which the new owner has with the property. Conveyancing is usually carried out by a solicitor, but other organizations, notably the House Owners' Co-operative Ltd., the Property Transfer Association and Homes, as well as the National House Owners' Society undertake the work and it is possible for an individual to do his own conveyancing if he so desires.

Co-ownership schemes After the end of the 1939–45 war, groups of people got together to provide cooperative housing, usually blocks of flats, to be bought on a rent-purchase basis. Thus were housing societies and associations formed, usually with a committee of management incorporating professional men including architects and surveyors who could give expert advice in their fields.

High interest rates and ever-rising building costs have made the homes which co-ownership schemes provided too expensive for those for whom they were primarily intended. Under existing arrangements therefore, housing associations and societies work closely with local authorities, the aim being to cater for those who fall into the gap between council tenants and owner-occupiers.

Several of the earlier associations continue to operate on a co-ownership basis under which residents have a share in the value of the home they occupy. See also **Housing Corporation**.

Cottages These can vary between two rooms and a kitchen and a seven-bedroom house, but they all have certain things in common.

These days, cash is the only way for most to buy a rural cottage as the lending institutions are generally committed to helping first-time buyers with modest homes or are further assisting those who are already owners to move into more modern houses.

Because of its age, the country cottage is never a subject on which to count for large building society or insurance company mortgages. Though some societies will entertain applications for loans, usually in the case of people buying as an alternative to an existing house, they like the more up-to-date properties on which values are more easily accountable.

Older properties which are acquired as first-time purchasers' only homes will rank for building society help where they are modernized to a proper degree but cottages which are second homes are broadly excluded from mortgage arrangements.

Rules however, do tend to be slightly flexible and some societies, notably those based locally, will consider mortgage applications on cottages, so the advice always is never to take the first 'No' for an answer and to shop around a bit.

Cash, on the other hand, is the key that can open a cottage door. Those able to proffer the money without having first to seek out methods of payment with the delay that that entails, find purchasing easy. The question is where to look for the cottage.

Siting is just as important where cottages are concerned as with any other home. There are demands for seclusion, remoteness, accessibility, and other priorities all of which mean different things to different people. To the city dweller a cottage in or on the outskirts of a village or hamlet will probably be considered suitable as a 'place in the country'. To the countryman, a country cottage may well mean the one house on a vast hillside or at the edge of a river in a valley.

Like houses, cottages come in all sizes, some so small as to be scarcely more than four walls divided across; others added to and improved to the point where they are cottages in name only. Cherry Cottage in suburbia may well turn out to be a six- or seven-bedroom home which would be a high-value property in anybody's estimation.

Petrol prices apart, the motorways have opened up new territories for cottage-hunting. Once situated too far distant in pre-motorway days because of the time taken to reach them, cottages just off these new high-speed routes are now sought. Owners consider less the mileage than the time taken to cover the distance. The same may be applied where major trunk road improvements have been carried out for the man with a weekend to spare can travel farther faster than ever before

It is true however, that petrol prices and cottage prices are inter related. The high cost of getting to some of the cottages has had the effect of trimming prices in a number of areas, but most affected appear to have been those within 15 miles of a town where owners have been obliged to travel in and out to work daily.

Cottages in traditionally popular regions have mainly been modernized so that it is difficult these days to discover one on which a buyer can execute his own plans. Some of the most derelict, seldom nothing more than shells, continue to have an appeal for that purpose, but most people are stuck with someone else's ideal.

For remoteness and shells perhaps Wales, the Yorkshire moors, parts of Cumbria and Northumbria, certainly some of the Scottish Highlands and Islands, will provide what is sought, and they may have also a fair area of land, an amenity much coveted these days. Doubtless the farm worker whose lot it once was to abide in these remote hovels is much more comfortably ensconced in a modern house in the nearest village with all amenities to hand!

Elsewhere, cottages can be found already partially or wholly modernized and there are areas to which it has been fashionable to go. Devon and Cornwall have always appealed to the Londoner and the man in the Home Counties with the result that cottages there have mostly been done up; likewise Worcestershire and Herefordshire and into Wales has attracted the Midlander; Wales too, is a venue for Merseyside, Tynesiders look to Cumbria and the Lake District, as do many from around Manchester; the Cotswolds lure people from everywhere, so do Scotland and the Islands, though obviously island cottages and those in more remote Highland regions call for a special type of owner.

Prices vary as widely as the cottages themselves. Sometimes it is possible to pick up a pair for knocking into a single home, occasionally even three or four have been incorporated for that purpose. At the other end of the scale one-bedroom/one-living room styles are by no means to be counted out. They are, to say the least, economical to heat, easy to run and maintain, light on rates and perfectly adequate for many a couple seeking an excuse not to put up relatives!

Council houses The Housing Act 1980 gave many secure tenants of local authorities and New Town Corporations the right to buy their homes at a discount of 33 per cent to 50 per cent, depending on the length of time the tenant has spent as a council tenant. This discount makes buying a council house or flat very attractive.

There is a maximum money value to the discount. Also the discounted slate price of a house or flat first occupied after April 1, 1974 must not be less than the cost of providing the house, including the cost of any improvements since that date.

The definition of 'secure' tenant is one who has been a council tenant for over three years, although that period need not have been continuous. There are exceptions; for example, where tenants are on land acquired by the council for future development, or tenancies to students and tenancies of less than a year provided for people who move to an area to take up employment.

The market value of the house or flat will be worked out by the local council, but the tenant has the right under the Act to appeal to the District Valuer if he thinks the value put on his home is too high.

Covenant Sometimes title deeds contain special provisions known as covenants which are usually restrictive. Covenants may rule that the purchaser of a particular property will not, for instance, sell off part of his garden to enable another house to be built on the site or, possibly, that where a single-storey property is concerned, it shall not be added to by building another floor.

D

Damp course A special layer inserted just above ground level in buildings to prevent dampness seeping into the walls. Many old houses were constructed without damp courses but in their cases the walls were sufficiently thick to keep most damp at bay. Early methods of damp coursing involved a double course of slates laid broken jointed and embedded in sand and cement. Today builders use a bituminous strip impregnated with lead. It is pliable and unless deliberately fractured, is tough to work with during building operations. More importantly it is very efficient.

Decoration The state of decoration of a house or flat may lead you to decide for or against buying it. Decorations are very much a personal matter and tastes differ. In these days, redecorating completely outside and inside before moving into a house or flat is an expensive operation and a property which is ready 'to walk into' is an attractive proposition even if the colours and styles are not exactly to your liking. These can be changed in due course when funds permit but meanwhile they serve the purposes of presenting a well-kept appearance to the outside world. Exterior paintwork should be renewed regularly to keep the woodwork in good repair.

Deeds These are legal documents which show details of ownership and other related aspects of a property. Previously deeds recorded transactions including grants, leases and redemptions or mortgages going back 30 years but the law now requires such details for only 15 years to be proved. The title deeds which provide evidence of any mortgagor's interest in a house or flat are retained by the mortgagee when the mortgage deed is executed. The arrangement ensures the mortgagee's interest is secured in the property for the loan which has been granted. The title deeds are returned when the mortgage is paid off, or redeemed as the phrase is. There is the established principle that a borrower who mortgages a freehold or leasehold interest as security for a loan shall retain ownership after the execution of a mortgage deed. The mortgage deed is merely an agreement between the borrower and the mortgagee of a promise to pay interest and repay the loan while at the same time, for the protection of the mortgagee, to undertake to maintain the property in good state of repair and insure it for its full value. The deed also contains the proviso that there can be possession by the mortgagee should the borrower fall down on his repayments.

Deposits Moneys put down by purchasers with either estate agents or solicitors during negotiations for acquiring a home. Deposits are strictly not necessary but are normally asked for as a token of good faith. They can vary between five and ten per cent or more of the purchase price of a property and are recognized as part of the purchase money when the time comes to pay over the total sum. Any deposits laid with estate agents should be clearly identified and a receipt obtained for them stating that the agent concerned is acting as stakeholder, thus establishing the fact that under normal circumstances the agent will be held liable for looking after the deposit and not the seller for whom the agent acts.

Because of the occasional dishonest agent controversy over deposits persists despite any observations, suggestions and proposals made. There is a considerable body of opinion among estate agents that they can and should handle money for clients and that those of repute do so in a careful, honest and straightforward way.

During 1976, the House of Lords ruled that the seller of a house should not be liable for the malfeasance of his estate agent. Their Lordships were brought into the scene when a county court and subsequently the Court of Appeal upheld the view that a seller of a house was liable to repay deposits paid by half a dozen potential purchasers to an estate agent acting for him who took off with the moneys.

In reversing the decisions of the lower courts, the House of Lords maintained that the loss of the deposits should be borne by the potential purchasers because the estate agent in law is not an agent for the seller since he does not have the power to enter into a contract on his behalf, nor to ask for or receive a deposit on behalf of the seller.

Buyers have protection over deposits if they conduct business only through agents whose firms are members of one of several recognized professional bodies including The Royal Institution of Chartered Surveyors (identified by the letters FRICS or ARICS); the Incorporated Society of Valuers and Auctioneers (FSVA or ASVA) or the National Association of Estate Agents (MNAEA). Firms where any of the partners or principles are entitled to carry these letters after their names are covered by indemnity schemes. The Royal Institution of Chartered Surveyors and the Incorporated Society of Valuers and Auctioneers have a joint indemnity scheme.

There is some disagreement too, on the actual amount of deposit. A contract for the sale and purchase will often provide for payment, usually of 10 per cent of the purchase price, to a stakeholder who is normally the seller's estate agent. There is a school of thought which presses the point that an agent would like to see, before that stage, a token deposit of £100 to show that the intentions of the purchaser are *bona fide*. When a deposit is paid it is returnable in full to the buyer in the event of a sale falling through before contracts are signed and exchanged. This deposit money is usually paid into the clients' account by an agent and, when a sale proceeds it will not be released to the seller without the express authority of the buyer through his solicitor if he has commissioned one to act for him, or on his personal authority if he is acting as his own lawyer.

Double glazing   Today when fuel costs are high, heat conservation in homes has assumed a major importance. Among methods advocated double glazing is prominent. Several firms specialize in fitting double glazing frames to existing windows and there are do-it-yourself kits for those so inclined. Problems associated with double glazing include condensation and in a number of types, difficulty in opening windows for a supply of fresh air. Newer procedures are overcoming initial irritations and there are double-glazed frames already assembled for installing in new buildings. Double glazing is considered of use too, as a sound insulator where homes are close to busy thoroughfares or near airfields. The practice is far from being universally accepted mainly because it prevents quick and easy opening and closing of windows as well as of cleaning them. There are firms which undertake made-to-measure frames which will be suitable for any type and size of window.

Draughts   House-purchasers are well advised to consider the design of a house, its situation in relation to the points of the compass and to the prevailing winds, the aspect of the rooms which are to be used most – on the north they can be less pleasant – and how the doors and windows are placed in relation to each other. Where a house has a front door and a back door linked only by a passage, draughts can be devastating. Similarly, doors and windows immediately opposite can cause discomfiture on a blustery day. With such built-in draughts, heating costs are in danger of escalating unless some means of excluding draughts can be devised. There are many efficient types of draught excluders, for both doors and windows available in hardware shops which even a modest handyman can fit without too much difficulty.

Dry rot   This is caused by a wood-destroying fungus which thrives on moist and stagnant air. Inadequate ventilation is usually a contributory factor. The fungus spores can be transported by numerous agents, including the wind and rot exists in many newly-built houses though latterly timbers are treated before being used. Red and white spots and red and black streaks give early signs that rot is present. As it progresses it can be detected by its objectionable, musty smell and the timber loses its resonance and starts to crumble. Boards which have been covered with linoleum are often affected. There are specialist firms dealing with rot and other timber problems and one of these can be called in to give advice and an estimate for remedial work. In bad cases the timbers affected will have to be cut out and replaced.

E

Easements   Technical term describing rights which owners of properties might exercise over those adjoining. Good examples are rights of way and rights of lights.

Edwardian   Homes built between 1900 and the outbreak of the First World War in 1914. They are found almost everywhere and can be in terraces, or are semi-detached and detached in their own grounds. In general they are less fussy and more utilitarian than their Victorian predecessors but provide equally spacious accommodation. The Edwardian businessman's house is smaller than that of his Victorian counterpart and the terrace homes of the era are larger than the Victorian rows which served what were then known as the working classes. Edwardian houses today modernize well and easily.

Electricity   Sellers and buyers of homes should give local electricity boards at least 24 hours' notice of intention to leave or take over a property. Sellers require meters to be read and it may be desirable for the supplies to be turned off at the mains. A purchaser will have to inform the electricity board when he requires the supplies to be restored.

Elizabethan   A sector of architecture of the Tudor period applicable to homes built in the reign of Elizabeth I between 1558 and 1603. Many of the largest country houses of the time are noted for their style, being constructed in E-shape around a courtyard. Smaller houses are in the 'black-and-white' design with exposed timbers and overhanging gables. They can be seen in many areas in the Home Counties and in Shropshire, Herefordshire, Worcestershire and Cheshire, and of course in Shakespeare's county, Warwickshire.

Estate agent   Person or partnership practising in the selling, buying, management and letting of property. Some are confined to house and flat selling and others cover, as well as residential property, commercial, industrial, shop and pub sectors of the market, handling also valuations' auctions, development advice, surveys, town planning and rating.

Most belong to one or other of the following organizations: The Royal Institution of Chartered Surveyors, The Incorporated Society of Valuers and Auctioneers, the National Association of Estate Agents, the Rating and Valuation Association. Some are not members of any organization and there is no bar to anyone's setting up as an estate agent. There are several well-respected firms whose principals are not qualified but who nevertheless conduct a proper and successful business.

For years various attempts have been made to control estate agents, the latest being for a system of registration. People will not be able to practise until they have satisfied certain conditions and had their name put on a register.

Membership of the bodies mentioned above entitles those concerned to use FRICS, ARICS, FSVA, ASVA, MNAEA and FRVA after their names. These bodies have professional examinations and have codes of conduct and safeguards to protect the public from malpractices. After qualifying, members of the bodies are known as associates (ARICS) and after some years in practice are made fellows (FSVA). Some firms describe themselves as surveyors, which in general terms is correct but they must not describe themselves as chartered surveyors unless they are members of the RICS. Not all chartered surveyors practice as estate agents.

Technically an agent is entitled to a fee for providing a valuation of the property if he is asked to do so, though many waive that charge if they are given the job of selling the property concerned.

If, at the same time, an agent is charged with finding another house or flat specifically, he would be justified in requesting a fee for his services in that direction. In practice he may already have on his books a property which could be acceptable to a seller seeking an alternative home in which case there would not be a fee. Agents act for clients, generally the sellers and must be instructed in proper terms if they are to be commissioned to look for a property for a buyer.

Exchange of contracts Contracts for home buying are in two identical parts, each signed by the seller and buyer. They exchange these parts at a particular stage in negotiations and the act binds them both legally to proceed with the transaction. Up to that point one or both may withdraw from the deal.

Extensions Rather than move some house-owners decide to extend an existing property, usually by adding another bedroom at the side or rear or by building over a garage, extending the loft, maybe pushing out a wall to enlarge a room or kitchen, or to create a second or bigger bathroom. With a freehold property an owner is able to make any alterations he wishes providing he obtains the necessary planning consent and complies with building regulations and local by-laws. In the case of a leasehold building the consent of the ground landlord must be given as well as the consents required from the local authority and planning body.

Planning consent will frequently involve also ensuring that neighbours have no objections; they have a case if a proposed extension would interfere with their privacy or possibly the views they enjoy. Where a house is being bought on mortgage the mortgagee's permission is also usually sought and given without ado as in any event a properly-executed extension will add to the value of a property anyway. The various permissions are necessary whether the owner intends doing the work himself or calls in an outside firm to do it for him. In some cases, extensions, if they can be classed as basic improvements, might qualify for some financial assistance by way of a loan or grant from the local authority.

There are firms specializing in executing the whole operation. They will prepare plans, obtain the necessary consents, apply for grants where applicable, and undertake any legal processes necessary as well as doing the actual building and fitting work, and will arrange some form of payment at the end of it all. Existing occupiers may however find that their building society or other lender will advance the money for extensions. An estate agent or surveyor with an architect's department will prepare plans and working drawings, obtain planning consents and so on as will an architect if he is employed to do so. The latter's charges are usually 10 to 20 per cent of the cost of the work which would include a certain amount of supervision of the job as well as the selection by tender of materials and a firm to carry out the extensions. Payment is usually by stages as the work is going along and it is customary for the house-owner to retain possibly about five per cent of the money for two or three months to ensure the job is completed satisfactorily. Sometimes it is preferable and cheaper to arrange for a bank loan or overdraft to pay for an extension rather than have the amount spread over a long term of years running parallel with an existing mortgage. A finance house will also usually be prepared to make a loan for the purpose of home improvement.

To help with choosing materials and providing general information the National Federation of Builders' and Plumbers' Merchants has set up a number of authorized home improvement centres. The centres are listed by the Federation in a leaflet available from their administrative office in London.

There are some 550 centres around the country, authorized and inspected by the Federation which has more than 1,000 member-firms representing 95 per cent of the merchants in Britain. The firms can supply most equipment and materials including bricks, cement, glass, gravel, paving, sand, timber and so on. With the supplies goes advice from painting a door to building an extension. There is also advice on financing projects.

Owners have to watch out for liability to Value Added Tax. VAT is payable on many home improvements but not if an improvement is deemed to be a major alteration of a building. There is however, no easy way of deciding what is a major alteration so it is generally a question to be thrashed out between a supplier and if necessary the VAT office.

F

Fences   It is said good fences make for good neighbours. Keep fences in good repair, but know which is yours. It is normally accepted that it belongs to the side on which the posts are set and it is usual for a householder to assume responsibility on those terms. However, it is not always the case and it is as well to find out from the deeds and accompanying plan where the boundary fences run and whose they are otherwise a person might find he is repairing someone else's. Fencing must not be dangerous to others; and in some districts there are restrictions on the heights to which a person may fence his property adjoining a highway. Generally there is no restriction on heights of fences between houses unless they were to reach such proportions that a right of light was infringed. If ditches or hedges rather than fences are the boundaries, the situation can be confused and often in the past resulted in lawsuits. Nowadays the exact limits are defined on the deeds.

Finding a Home   Hard head rather than soft heart is a necessary ingredient in home finding. The first major decision to come to is what can be afforded, not what is preferred. The amount of money available and to be called upon can very well not only dictate what can be acquired but also where. Most people buy a home with the aid of a mortgage and anyone proposing to ask a building society for a loan should have established a savings pattern with it. Societies react more favourably to those who are known as 'members' that is, investors, than to outsiders who really only qualify for aid when coffers are overflowing. There is a variety of properties from which to make a choice again depending upon how much there is to spare and attention should be paid to the proximity of essential services, shops and schools, churches and other places of community interest as well as to the distances involved in travelling to and from work.

Fixtures   When selling a property, items such as baths, washbasins, radiators and boilers, which are attached to a house by screws or pipes are assumed to be part of the deal unless they are specifically excluded in the contract. Sometimes light fittings and other items which are suited only for the purpose and places they occupy are included. It is assumed that items standing by their own weight, such as refrigerators, gas and electric cookers, portable heaters and so on are not part of the property in the same way as the attached items are.

Flat Accommodation, usually in a block and on one floor but with a common main entrance. Flats may be what are known as 'purpose-built' or in conversions created from an existing house or houses. They are distinct from maisonettes which may be on one or two floors but which have their own separate entrances from outside.

Freehold Term used to define the status of a property. The owner of a freehold property owns the land and buildings on it outright as distinct from a leasehold under which a house or other building is held on a rented basis from the landowner or freeholder. In Scotland, the free-holder is the person who feus or leases land to others for building purposes. The rent paid to him is called feu duty. The feu system is being abolished; as each Scottish house subject to feu is sold, the seller is required to redeem the feu.

With a freehold house or bungalow, an owner is literally not committed to payments to anyone except those required by law, such as rates and taxes. Mortgages are normally reasonably easy to obtain on freeholds, though they are not difficult where leases of 99 or 999 years are concerned either. Conditions of being granted a mortgage however, may require the buyer of a freehold property to undertake certain maintenance and repairs and with the consent of the mortgagee a freeholder can execute alterations to his property. In some parts free-holds are subject to what are known as rent charges which in practice operate as a perpetual rent to the ground landlord. Rent charges are common in the Manchester area and these are periodic charges on the land on which a house stands. They are usually only nominal.

Some blocks of flats are also sold on a freehold basis, but in such cases that will be on condition that buyers' rights are safeguarded by their being in a residents' association which will assume responsibility for the bricks and mortar as well as for the efficient running of the building from day to day. In the early 1900s and towards the start of the last war in 1939, several private estates were developed. Sometimes a builder constructed several house types on such estates, in other cases plots were sold off to individuals who then commissioned their own houses on them. A few estates were developed by several builders each producing a series of homes of different styles. It was usual in the case of private estates to have overall supervision, often by installing gates at entrances. Residents were then surcharged for the upkeep of roads and porterage, along with other expenses which varied according to the work undertaken. Most estates were, and still are, subject to covenants. These stipulated a wide range of conditions. Many covenants prevent more than one house being built on an acre; some restrict plots to half an acre or less. Other covenants indicated either the size or style of building to be erected, or its minimum cost. In all cases the idea was to maintain an estate at a certain standard and to attract residents well able to afford relatively large houses.

Since the last war, many covenants have been challenged in the courts and some have been set aside by judges. The reason for either cancelling or modifying covenants has been that because there is a shortage of land it is unreasonable to maintain estates where only one house may be built on an acre. In urban areas as many as 16 or 20 homes have been constructed per acre, and, where flats are concerned, many more.

Purchasers of new houses and flats will find that there are certain additional items to be agreed compared with secondhand homes. Most of these are to do with roads to be constructed as well as with the boundaries to be created until the local authority adopts them. Contracts will also mention building defects and the fact that the National House-Building Council's rules and regulations about these will apply where the builder or developer is a registered member of that body. It is usual these days for a builder to be a member of the Council because unless he is building societies are reluctant to grant mortgages; in fact some decline altogether where a Council certificate of good workmanship is not available.

It is, in the case of new homes, likely that a standard form will be issued by the builder's solicitors to buyers and deviation from it is not normally permitted.

G

Garage It was fashionable in prewar days to refer to the garage as the motor-house! Then it was frequently built at some distance from the house itself, often at the extreme end of the rear garden so that the car could be run on to the road at the back and brought round to the front. With the gradual demise of the spacious garden and other considerations, among them the fact that today's car-owner likes his car to be as near to his front door as he can get it, garages are sometimes integral parts of the house itself or very close to it either attached or just detached. Modern methods of living as well as a more affluent society have demanded double garages and in some cases garaging for three or more vehicles, though a car port suffices in most cases to provide shelter and cover for additional family vehicles.

Garden buildings Most houses are incomplete without some form of outside building, be it a shed or a greenhouse, pavilion or garden frame. Specialists in garden buildings abound and the range includes greenhouses in aluminium or wood, conservatories, summerhouses and garden sheds of various designs.

Owners of greenhouses and sheds will always tell you that they wish they had bought a bigger one when they originally decided to have one! Size indeed, depends upon what it is proposed the individual owner intends to do with or in it. That means that careful selection is essential in the first place and it is a splendid idea to take lots of time to go around the many display areas offering garden products. Styles and materials as well as plans vary considerably and manufacturers have everything from rustic, deal, cedar and other woods to glass fibre.

A first approach might be to send for one of the several booklets on the subject prepared by suppliers and manufacturers. For instance, Guildhall Garden Products has a series of free packs. These include those giving advice on siting greenhouses and details of ranges of garden sheds and other garden buildings. Advice is also available from F. Pratten & Co.

One of the latest aids to greenhouse heating is a Shilton product, information on which may be obtained from the firm's headquarters or at stores, garden centres, gas showrooms or Calor gas dealers. It is a free-standing stove without chimney, wicks, tanks or ashes and is approved by the gas authorities. Models are available for natural gas or bottled gas and there are two sizes, approximately $1\frac{1}{2}$ kw and $2\frac{3}{4}$ kw.

Gardens For many home ownership provides them with a garden for the first time in their lives. Knowing the difference between a weed and a flower is not always that simple, nor is there any disgrace in such a lack. Help from many sources is valuable and many seedsmen willingly supply catalogues in which are hints on growing things. In conjunction with the expanded towns, Greater London Council has been producing a booklet to help householders on new estates to design and run their gardens. The booklet is available from the information officer at the Department of Agriculture & Civic Design.

Gas Along with electricity, gas boards should be notified at least 24 hours in advance by owners either vacating or moving into a property. For those going out, meters will be read and bills made to the day of leaving. Omitting to do this could mean being charged for gas which the next occupier is using!

Georgian During the years of the Georges between 1714 and 1820, many homes and other buildings followed a certain style of which the Adams were leading exponents. The Georgian style of architecture has never gone out of fashion and indeed is copied successfully today. It is a 'no-fuss' type of construction with simplicity the keynote. The larger houses usually are adorned by the addition of a portico in the

Grecian style. Windows are long with small panes and often reach the full height of a wall from ceiling to floor; rooms are well-proportioned and of generous dimensions.

Gothic While the true Gothic period of architecture spanned the years from 1190 to 1550 the end of the 18th century witnessed an offshoot form, the best-known of which is the Strawberry Hill villa. The style breaks with the classical architecture and ordered arrangement of the Georgian styles and was favoured by the successful manufacturers of the day and is seen in their highly decorated and sprawling mansions. Many of the houses created at the time were the brainchild of the individual moneyed businessman who paid little real attention to style but leaned towards Gothic as being an impressive building in a heavy, solid way, reflecting his own determined methods.

Granny flat Sometimes it is possible to meet the needs of elderly relatives by altering a sufficiently large property to create entirely separate self-contained accommodation . . . a granny flat. Many couples who wish parents to be close to but not among them find the granny flat a solution. It provides the elderly with a home of their own but where sons and/or daughters can keep an eye on them in case of emergencies. Numbers of couples have discovered that it has been possible to purchase the type of property which adapts in this way relatively cheaply and, with the help of funds from mother or father (or both), have been able to meet the costs of establishing a granny flat. Often in larger houses, former staff accommodation is easily improved for the purpose.

Grants Local authorities are empowered to give grants to owners who wish to install basic amenities in an older house. Grants are sometimes accompanied by a loan to enable the owner to carry through the work required. There are three types of grant; standard, discretionary and special. The first covers the installation of a fixed bath or shower, washbasin, sink, inside w.c. and a hot-and-cold water system. There is provision for the grant to cover up to half the cost of installing these basic amenities.

Discretionary grants are given where certain works are considered necessary to bring a house up to modern standards and again up to half the cost is generally available. Frequently a standard grant and a discretionary grant can be obtained where an owner can prove his case.

There is a further payment where the owner of a property having three or more floors intends to convert the building to flats and special grants, again at the discretion of the council, are intended to improve houses which are shared where several rooms may be tenanted but the properties are not converted into flats.

Recently local authorities have altered previous policies of clearance of sub-standard properties and are giving grants for the rehabilitation of them. In areas where many old houses form a major sector of the stock, local authorities are generous in their interpretation of the regulations. Anyone contemplating the acquisition of a property at present lacking standard amenities should not count on a loan and/or grant without proper consultation with the local authority officials concerned. Grants are not automatic and need for them must be shown.

Ground rent   Regular payment made by a person holding a lease, the leaseholder, to the ground landlord, the freeholder; leasehold properties are subject to ground rents of anything between £2 a year for very old homes to £1,000 for a luxury penthouse in London. An average ground rent for a modern three-bedroom home would be around £20 a year. Payments may be made annually or quarterly. Leases are granted for any period above three years. Flats are normally subject to leases of 99 years though there are some with leases of 40 or 50 years; some new homes are on leases for 999 years.

Guesthouses   For those who like open spaces but not necessarily in the country or up a mountainside there are guesthouses and small hotels at the coast. Again the line of demarcation between a guesthouse and an hotel is not clearly defined, nor is it between a guesthouse and a boarding house. Many people who have spent pleasant holidays in a resort town make up their minds that when they 'retire' they will take over a place on the front. These small guesthouses and boarding houses as well as the hotels, are usually run as family concerns. Because of the numbers of rooms involved they are cheaper to purchase than, say a three- or four-bedroom home on or just off the promenade and from which are panoramic views of the sea. Some of the smaller properties close to the front are, along with some country places, also pressed into service as 'bed and breakfast' concerns, again producing a welcome income for owners who are prepared to put up with strangers in the night and/or during the day in their homes.

H

Ha-ha   Some of the older properties have a hedge, fence or wall sunk between slopes. This feature, known as a ha-ha, is a prized gardening division. It is often used as an ornamental barrier between lawns and say, a vegetable patch, as a natural or man-made break providing a visual mark of individuality.

Hardwood   Timber which includes oak, ash, walnut, mahogany, teak, ebony and rosewood. They are all deciduous trees mainly having broad leaves.

Heating There is a never-ending quest for the most efficient form of heating; not everyone succumbs to the fashion for some type of central heating. English, and Scottish, families, particularly the distaff side, like to see what they call 'the flame' and so demand an open solid-fuel burning fire. Great strides have been made in providing solid fuels of varying quality for household use including those used in stoves and slow-burning grates in smokeless zones.

Competing fuels are gas, oil and electricity, using convectors and radiators. There is a wide range from which to choose and the ultimate decision is a personal one to be left to the householder. Generally, though not by any means precisely, coal is the least expensive but tends to be not only the dirtiest but also the most troublesome fuel, and electricity the most expensive but also the cleanest.

Quickly making an impression is solar heating and experiments carried out in the summer of 1976 when the sun shone more days than ever before since meteorologists had maintained records, were completely successful. At Telford New Town, two systems of solar heating were installed, one, forming the front porch costing £200 and the other set in the roof and costing £400 at the time. The Telford experiments, scheduled to last a year, seemed to justify provisional plans that the systems should be installed in new homes being built, with priority being given to elderly residents for whom free hot water would be available from solar sources. The experiments indicate that a saving in heat costs of 40 per cent for an average family would be possible. Tests in a standard house produced steady supplies of hot water up to 160°F and most people would have bathed without any water heating costs. Other experiments have prompted the installation of solar heating panels in a holiday-lodge scheme in Scotland at Loch Rannoch, where even in February quite encouraging results were being obtained using what sunlight there was for ancillary heating purposes. While ambitious experiments are also proceeding to use the sun in space equipment to provide the Earth with all the energy it required for ever, as far as the more ordinary trials are concerned, the main problems are associated not with the production of heat but of storing it satisfactorily so that the best use may be made of it. As well as obtaining solar energy from 'skylights' in house roofs, solar heating systems have been successfully employed in raising and maintaining the temperature in swimming pools.

Hereditament Commonly used in Scotland regarding houses and flats. It means real property which may be inherited.

Home inspections Most people seeking a house or flat get a 'feeling' about a particular place and in fact, all things subsequently being equal almost make up their minds then and there that 'this is for them'. Having got the feeling, there are a few spot checks which can be made before a proper structural survey is embarked upon. There are the obvious things, the measurements of various rooms, how much storage space there is, the question of whether or not the doors are sufficiently wide to allow through large items of furniture if these are possessed and that goes for the staircase too, which ought not to be too steep.

The atmosphere in a house or flat will indicate much; dampness has a habit of penetrating those not used to it; a comfortable steady temperature indicates that the heating is working well. Where there is gas it should not reveal its presence by its smell! Upstairs in the bathroom, dripping taps, discoloured spots where the drips have dropped and any chips out of the bath or washbasin tend to indicate some neglect unless there is a sound reason in an otherwise obviously well-maintained property. Make some excuse to flush the lavatory and notice how much noise emanates from the refilling of the cistern. Similarly, notice any noise after running a bath tap for some time. If the property is close to a main road, open a window and listen to the traffic noise. Close it to ascertain how effectively it keeps out the sounds.

Such an inspection can also include a casual discussion with the owner as to fixtures and fittings and which items he may or may not be inclined to remove. A tape measure can be handy if one wishes to measure up sizes of windows for curtains and floors for carpets though these are often the bits and pieces which a buyer can agree to take over with the property for an agreed small additional sum.

In your haste to approve of the interior don't forget there is an external aspect to the whole business. Apart from garden sheds and greenhouses the property should be considered in relation to its neighbours and to any unsightly buildings which may be in close proximity. A glance at the roof will sometimes show any defects although with the exception of missing slates or tiles a specialist in the field should eventually be called in to check on that. It will however, be possible to see whether or not anything which should be attached, possibly a television aerial or a chimney brace, is really attached and not ready to drop off! Badly-hung garage doors will reveal their own defects as will collapsing fences. With a bit of luck the latter will belong to the man next door! It's a good idea to check that it does. Watch where the sun strikes during the day; it could make all the difference to the produce from the garden.

Homesteading This is a term used to describe the sale of unimproved dwellings by local authorities and other bodies. The price asked for these homes reflects their condition. In London the Greater London Council had 800 applicants for 60 properties offered for homesteading in 1980. Building societies are looking favourably at this kind of sale.

Housing Corporation The Housing Corporation's function is to assist housing associations to provide homes where they are most needed; previously, associations and societies undertook schemes wherever they considered them desirable.

Since the passing of the 1974 Housing Act, all housing associations have come under the umbrella of the Housing Corporation, which has its headquarters in Tottenham Court Road, London, and regional offices in London, Croydon, Surrey, and Potters Bar, Herts., covering the South-East, Exeter for the South-West, Cardiff for Wales, Wolverhampton for the West Midlands, Leicester for East Midlands, Manchester for the North-West, Leeds for the North-East and Edinburgh for Scotland.

The Corporation lends funds to associations, with emphasis on those operating in the main areas of housing stress, such as city centres, and high on the priority lists are societies meeting the special needs of single persons, the disabled, the elderly and others whose requirements are not met by local authorities. Only associations registered by the Corporation can qualify for funds, which in fact are provided by the taxpayer.

Set up by Parliament in 1964 the Housing Corporation has a management board appointed by the Government and borrows its funds from the Treasury.

In the case of new lettings, rents are fixed by rent officers and there can also be joint mortgages with local authorities where elderly people are concerned. Actively under consideration for some time has been some form of cooperative housing which would be based on accommodation being available on both an investment and rental participation. As an example a person or couple able to afford say 30 per cent of a share of the capital cost of a block of flats would be able to pay the balance of 70 per cent as rent.

In total there are more than 5,500 housing associations of various types and sizes operating throughout the British Isles. The major activity centres on about 200 of the largest. Some of them have schemes under which a life-lease is sold. On death or surrender the cost of the lease is repaid so that heirs are not deprived of their inheritance. In a project by the Retirement Lease Housing Association flats and bungalows built were subject to leases costing between £14,700 and £20,600. On surrender of these leases, they revert to the association which then reallocates the accommodation at the market price ruling at the time. A maintenance charge covers essential repairs and general cleaning and the association mainly caters for those who find the effort of running a house and garden beyond their capabilities but who nevertheless wish to retain some independence and to live among their personal belongings. They are also in this way able to preserve their capital from the sale of a family home instead of spending it on rent or hotel bills. As an added bonus, the association appoints wardens to oversee the inhabitants in case of emergencies. Suitability or otherwise of applicants is determined by the association which has under way other schemes of a similar nature.

Sometimes there are opportunities to buy into existing co-ownership schemes, when it is usual for a buyer to acquire another's share and pay rent and it is possible too, for a group of like-minded individuals to approach a building society for a mortgage to carry through a scheme of their own on some form of co-ownership basis. These however, are usually confined to the conversions of large houses into smaller units, possibly with additions. In such cases, where they are approved, the Housing Corporation may decide to guarantee a loan.

Under the 1974 Act if a housing association wishes to borrow from the Housing Corporation it can only do so after it is registered. The process of registration does not cost an association anything but it does give the Corporation the opportunity to scrutinize members of management committees and to check on activities.

Parallel with the Housing Corporation is the Federation of Housing Associations which acts as an advisory body. It organizes various programmes including those for management training and investment procedures and the like. Not only does it negotiate on behalf of housing associations as a whole but it also acts as a liaison between the Corporation, Government and local authorities.

Individual associations have their own methods of allocating accommodation; some maintain a waiting list, others work through housing aid centres and other local organizations concerned with housing and welfare; many operate on a combination of the two.

Under the Housing Act 1980 some housing association tenants have the right to acquire their homes.

I

Improvements Most home-owners consider improvements to their properties from time to time. Before it was considered important to preserve, from an economic as well as an aesthetic point of view, some of the older houses, official policy was to sweep away outdated buildings. Today local authorities give every encouragement to those who wish to improve houses by installing amenities considered not only desirable but necessary for modern living and there are grants and loans to help those undertaking the task.

While improvements are not always extensions many of them to be done properly do involve additional building or major alterations to existing walls. That being so it should be cleared with the local authority whether the work to be done does or does not require planning consent. In any case it will have to comply with building by-laws and regulations, and guidance on the fact is freely available from council officials.

Few homes are not improved by the addition, however modest, of a porch. This can of course, vary in size and style, and from the point of view of heating it can be of great benefit. As it protects what were previously exterior doors, a porch conserves a good deal of heat which would otherwise be lost on opening the front or back door. A bonus, depending upon how much glass is used in its construction, is its usefulness as a conservatory in which a few, or indeed many, plants can be raised and kept. Not an inconsiderable number of owners have ripened a fair crop of tomatoes in the porch!

Where a glassed-in porch may not be possible, an open lean-to can also help. Such an addition can keep some of the worst weather off the entrance and where space is available can be extended over a garage entrance to form a carport.

A warning – do not let such appendages become cluttered up with bits and pieces overflowing from the inside of the house. They can easily and quickly give the place a dejected and forlorn look as well as continually getting in the way of what are more essential uses.

More ambitious improvements might be the introduction of a second bathroom or shower room where space permits, or the erection of one of the shower cabinets which surprisingly fit exceedingly small corners. While not everyone approves washbasins in bedrooms can also add to convenience, especially if there are elderly persons in the house or, where there are large families with everyone trying to get out together to catch buses and trains, so that calls made on the bathroom are cut to the bone.

Insulation In these days of high costs for fuel, efficient insulation of properties is vital. Much can be done by a householder himself; he can obtain a proprietary brand of insulating material for the roof space. More heat is lost to a house through the roof than in any other way and laying strips of glass fibre between the rafters is an efficient method of dealing with the situation. Almost monthly, new forms of fillings for cavity walls are being introduced and recent styles of double glazing, though they do not prevent heat loss to the degree always claimed for them, are simpler, more efficient and attractive than the older forms, many of which caused condensation and cleaning problems.

Interest rates Borrowing to buy a home is subject to interest on the amount of the loan. From time to time, according to the rate recommended for banks by the Bank of England, the Building Societies' Association will suggest what the rates of interest should be for home-buyers having loans from its member societies. Changes in Bank Rate do not automatically mean any alteration in building society rates though they do have a bearing on them long-term.

Societies implement two rates of interest – one is given to investors who, as they have alternative sources for their moneys expect to be given a return on their investments at least as good as they can obtain anywhere else; the other is the rate charged to borrowers. For some time it was between 10 and 11 per cent for borrowing and $6\frac{1}{2}$ to 7 per cent for investing. Insurance companies and local authorities which also advance funds for house purchase invariably charge at fixed rates for the whole term of a mortgage while building societies often vary theirs. An insurance company or council will also charge a little more, possibly a quarter per cent above the ruling building society rate at the time of granting a loan. Borrowing from a bank, say short term for a change of house, is subject to whatever rate of interest is applicable at various times during the period of the loan. The current (1981) mortgage interest rate of 14·5 per cent will come under pressure to fall as soon as the Minimum Lending Rate is reduced from 16 per cent.

Insurance Insurance is one of those payments made in the hope it will never be needed! Apart from personal insurance it is usually advised that policies should be taken out to cover the fabric and contents of a house, as well as for mortgage protection. Most professional men will advise a man aged about 30 taking out a loan of about £15,000 to cover his undertaking with a mortgage protection insurance of around £8,000 just 'in case'. There are also methods of covering loans by endowment insurances either with or without profits at the end of the term of the mortgage. Non-profit endowments wipe off the loan without any bonus to the policyholder at the end of the mortgage term; with-profit endowments usually provide the policyholder with a bonus, depending upon how the company's business has gone over the years. Mortgage protection insurance, subject to tax relief, costs for £15,000, about £35 a year gross, though of course the actual amount depends upon the age of the insured.

Insurance on the building itself is about 75p per £500 with a minimum of £5 or £6 and special rates for more than £25,000. Contents insurance varies between £3 and £4 to £9, but there are special rates for valuable items separately listed. Most insurers charge higher rates for houses in the Greater London area.

Island homes Going to an island to live demands a certain type of person. In a word, island living is by no means everyone's cup of tea. Though Britain itself is an island, it is large enough to take care of those who need a fairly extensive land mass, but selecting one or other of the scores of islands around our coasts is quite another matter.

It is possible nonetheless, to go to an island which though very 'English' is still almost abroad. In this respect the Channel Islands spring to mind, and with them the Isle of Wight and the Isle of Man. While being very 'British' the Channel Islands and the Isle of Man each have their own administrations and tax laws, so there are some advantages in living in them, but against that there are drawbacks insofar as accessibility is concerned and the fact that they can be restrictive for anyone used to wide open spaces.

As far as the Channel Islands are concerned, with the exception of Alderney, residential restrictions are operative and in any case there are relatively few homes to buy and, as a consequence, those which are available are very expensive. Guernsey and Jersey's administrators

113

are well aware that too much pressure and too much money could squeeze out the local inhabitants from the market and so there are measures to protect them.

Alderney's administration is controlled by Guernsey and the attractions include a low rate of income tax and the absence of surtax or death duty.

On all the islands the older properties are clustered in the streets of the main towns. Where there has been development since 1950 it is generally in traditional British style in small schemes on the outskirts of existing communities.

Unlike the Isle of Wight, which is administratively under Hampshire, the Isle of Man has its own laws and parliament. Apart from being a self-governing community within the Commonwealth but not constitutionally part of the United Kingdom, it has a scenic appeal similar to that of Scotland. There are hills and valleys with streams and the coast is everywhere within easy reach.

Building societies to not operate on the Isle of Man and the only loan schemes are those under the aegis of the Manx government which are sometimes available to individuals or companies wishing to house key workers.

Like the Isle of Wight and certain islands close to the West Coast of Scotland, the Isle of Man is well served by sea and air transport with regular services connecting with the principal ports and towns on the mainland. An advantage which the Isle of Man has which is sometimes absent in other islands is that all its towns and villages have piped water, electricity and drainage and in addition a number of places have gas. Schools are plentiful and there is a reciprocal health service with Britain's. Much has been done locally on Man to attract people to retire there and to establish second homes, and there have been attempts too to take light industry to the island so that there is work for the younger elements of the population.

For many years few new homes were built on Man, but during the late 1960s and 1970s there was a spate of building, including bungalows and flats, the latter mainly with sea views at Ramsey.

Man is fairly easily divided as far as residential matters are concerned; in the northern half are the majority of older higher-value homes with the less expensive properties being found in the southern arc. Proximity to main transport means that Douglas, popular with holidaymakers and the administrative centre for the island, has become the residential pivot on which prices turn. Planes to Douglas from London, Newcastle upon Tyne, the Midlands, Liverpool and Manchester take less than an hour. From Liverpool by ferry takes around 3½ hours.

Within very easy travelling on the island is a wide variety of property. Manx cottages, sometimes with up to two acres or substantial period properties in 20 or 30 acres with everything in between, are possible buys. After 1945 until new building started, purchasers had little except the very old and Victorian properties from which to choose. Popular buys are former fishermen's cottages, now modernized, at the water's edge and double-fronted Manx houses on or near one of the island's harbours or overlooking the sea.

For those desirous of building a home to their own plans, the Isle of Man does have sites available from time to time. The best of these are expensive by any standards and none is what might be called cheap.

Homes on the Isle of Wight too, find their prices governed somewhat by their proximity to ferry services operating between Yarmouth and Lymington, Portsmouth and Fishbourne and Southampton and Cowes. The journey takes between 30 and 50 minutes and some of the timings are regulated by the seasons.

At the same time, the island, like the Isle of Man, is a very self-contained community, with the bulk of the population in the east. Another factor impinging on prices is how close or how distant homes are from the towns, and yachting centres are favoured with a consequent hardening of figures, particularly for waterfront properties and the best-kept period houses. Taken all round, Yarmouth is the most expensive area in which to buy, Cowes and Newport, the capital, providing some of the least expensive properties, though houses with water frontage anywhere have that fact reflected in prices.

Among the easiest islands to reach from the mainland is Anglesey, which provides much of the best residential content for those whose employment is in Bangor, North Wales, and again, waterside properties are at a premium.

Less favoured at least by the masses, are the Scilly Isles reached in just under three hours by steamer from Penzance to St Mary's, the principal town. There is also an air service. Only occasionally on the Isles of Scilly are there homes to buy and prices for these are generally negotiable. Occasional new building has gone on as is the case on Anglesey, but the potential home-owner on both is broadly limited to an existing older-style property.

Services to islands around the Scottish coast, can be few and far between and a sea crossing can take up most of the day. Air ferries to Orkney and Shetland, Lewis and Harris, Uist and Barra, Islay and Tiree, cut travelling time to main centres, and handle emergencies generally. Some services are suspended in winter.

Most quickly accessible are islands closest to the mainland. Near Glasgow is Arran and Bute, farther north, Mull and Skye.

While it is possible to buy modern homes on some of the islands, the principal demand is for a cottage or smallholding. These are available from extremely low prices for some of the remotest and most primitive buildings, but possibly with an acre of ground. There are, too, crofting estates of several thousand acres with well-modernized cottages; the substantial houses presiding over them are legacies from past days when some of the islands were owned by one or two people or were in single ownership, as indeed some of the smaller ones still are. The islands almost without exception, provide many sporting facilities, notably fishing, and estates on them are sought for that reason.

J

Jacobean A style in architecture and furniture associated with the period between 1603 and 1688 during the reign of James I and James II. Houses built during those years are without frills but well-proportioned and are best known for their plaster work and panelling, which is usually heavy and in oak. Jacobean staircases are renowned for their splendid carving.

Joint ownership Properties may be bought by two or more purchasers in a joint arrangement. All equally own the whole and the rights to a house or flat are fully enforceable when a sale occurs. It is common these days for husband and wife to enter into joint ownership so that liability to tax is lessened in the event of the death of one of them. The share of the house or flat is therefore half what it would otherwise be were there no joint ownership and any tax liability is levied on the value of the half.

Joists The timbers supporting floorboards and ceilings. Susceptible to wet and dry rot if not properly ventilated, they have to be replaced if attacked by rot or by woodworm. If a floor is badly affected it may be necessary not only to renew the boards but the joists as well.

K

Keep A relic of medieval days. The keep was the central portion of a castle and became the last refuge for a garrison in the event of attack. Small keeps are still to be seen in some of the Norman buildings which have been preserved as homes, though it is doubtful whether they are truly genuine and copies have been made from time to time by eccentrics. Keeps are most common in Scotland, in family castles dating from the days of incessant raids by warring clans.

Key Architecturally, a central stone, the keystone, at the apex of an arch which locks together the component parts.

Key money A form of premium demanded, illegally as it happens, from a prospective occupier of a house or flat, to enable him to obtain vacant possession. It has been known for an occupant of a property to demand key money, which he contends he has to pay to someone else, as the price for leaving his present accommodation.

Keys It is sometimes possible for a purchaser to obtain the keys to a seller's property before he has actually bought it (i.e. actually paid over the money). Such arrangements should not be entered into without proper safeguards and a solicitor will discuss adequate protection for the parties in such circumstances. Estate agents retain keys and there must be a proper arrangement when the time comes for handing over and receiving keys. Where a seller has yet to be paid, it is vital that his rights are protected if the key is to be released to the purchaser.

King post The vertical beam at the apex of a pair of rafters seen in some of the older well-preserved period houses. Properties retaining king posts are considered a feather in the cap of those owning them.

Kitchens The kitchen plays an important part in the smooth running of the home and yet only too often it is a badly designed and depressing place in which to work.

One of the quickest ways to give the kitchen a new look is to change the sink unit. There are several types on the market and it is possible to find one which not only improves the look of the kitchen but is also of greater use to the distaff side. Modern homes have suffered to some extent having relatively small kitchens which restricts what alternatives can be accomplished but there is always something. Larger, older houses where kitchens were once the spacious domain of the Mrs Bridges of this world, lend themselves to endless permutations. There will most certainly be a chimney breast, which in these days of central heating, might well be removed to provide even more space which can be better utilized. In both modern and old kitchens, a well-laid floor, as colourful or subdued as is desired, lends a completely new air.

With the modern wife holding down a job as well as running a house, a kitchen often needs to double up as a breakfast room, so, depending upon space, a table is a must and there are ingenious examples which fold away, drop down, become cupboard doors or otherwise disguise themselves. Whichever an owner chooses should meet his individual and his family's needs. A 'bar' style along one wall, with high stools, may be the answer in some cases, the stools being tucked away under the counter when not in use. The larger kitchens will certainly provide space for a separate eating division; in smaller versions it will have to be assimilated as best it can.

These days manufacturers are also going in for more colour and one is able to buy 'sets' to match, with cooker, fridge, washing machine, dishwasher and so on matching or contrasting with cupboards and other equipment. Heed should be paid however, to the actual functional capabilities of any equipment. Easy-clean, quickly assembled gadgets are preferable to those with protruding bits and pieces which are awkward to handle and time-consuming in preparation and dismantling to say nothing of the dirt- and grease-carrying capacities of some frills and patterns. Among incidentals there are taps which are not only attractive but are easily manipulated by the arms when hands are full. Most kitchens can benefit from a few strategically-placed cupboards. These may be bought all ready to hang up on a soundly-prepared series of hooks or screws, they may be constructed by the handy man or they may be fitted by a carpenter into convenient nooks and crannies or above work surfaces. Height is an important consideration; it is pointless to have them out of reach of the tiny wife of a tall husband. Where possible it is better for cupboards to be hand or shoulder high as both stooping and stretching is a wearying business for those who are continually fetching and carrying. A spot check will also indicate where a shelf or two can be handy, particularly for the cookery books and other relevant information in the kitchen – the emergency numbers for the electricity and gas people, the water authority and the oil company, the cards for meter readings, fuse wire.

Time is well spent too, studying the placing of equipment; the washing machine, refrigerator, dishwasher, deep-freeze and so on, as well as the suitability or otherwise of the sink. Obviously, the washing machine, used less than the others, can be well out of the way; the dishwasher and fridge, used all the time, need to be on hand.

Those interested in completely reshaping their kitchen can do worse than consult a specialist in the sphere. One of these, Servoplan Kitchens undertakes to do a complete job in less than a fortnight. The service embraces designing and installing a new kitchen at an all-inclusive price for which estimates are given free. The company's plans are based on making the best use of the existing kitchen premises and everything is included from units required to plumbing, wiring, tiling, floors and decorating as well as new cookers and washing machines and other equipment if desired.

L

Land certificate   Issued to a registered owner of a home which has a registered title. It shows what details are entered on the register of that property at the Land Registry. A mortgaged property does not qualify for a land certificate but a charge certificate is issued to the mortgagee.

Landlord Generally what the intending home owner is trying to get away from! Letting for profit is a dubious enterprise hedged about with restrictions, but it may at some time be necessary for a home owner to become a landlord so the various problems and ways to avoid them are discussed under Letting.

Land Registry The Government department in which details of the registration of title to a property is maintained.

In technical terms, land is either registered or it is not. If it is, then the procedure of change of ownership involves transferring it; if it is not, then the procedure is one of conveyancing.

Over the years, districts have been designated registration districts and a registry set up. When a house is sold in a district which has become a registration district since the house was last sold, it is registered. In such cases the deeds of the house are sent to the Land Registry after the transactions have been completed. In turn the Land Registry issues a certificate which takes the place of the deeds.

First registrations are less costly than subsequent dealings. On a property valued at £10,000 the Land Registry fee for a first registration is £14·40 and for subsequent dealings £21·60. Registration however, invariably means a saving in legal costs for a purchaser. Where the benefit accrues to the seller is that once his property is registered he has no difficulty in proving he is the owner and is able to authorize the buyer or his solicitor to inspect his title to it in the register.

It is policy to extend registration to the whole country in due course, a decision made in 1965. Some areas were registration districts before that date, including Kent and Surrey and most boroughs within Greater London.

There are Land Registry offices at Croydon, Durham, Gloucester, Harrow, Lytham St Annes, Nottingham. Plymouth, Stevenage, Swansea and Tunbridge Wells. A call to any of the offices will elucidate whether or not a particular town or county is a registration district thus indicating the status of any house in that district.

As far as registration is concerned there is no difference between leasehold and freehold; both are registered if they are in a registration area and there will be a land certificate relating to them.

Until registration catches up on all properties, many houses are on unregistered land. That means that instead of a land certificate which contains all the relevant details about ownership and whether or not there are any mortgages and so on, there will be deeds giving details about ownership going back 15 years at least. Up to the passing of the Law of Property Act in 1969 a seller was required to produce title deeds, i.e. conveyances, for 30 years previous to a sale. If a leasehold is involved a seller is required also to produce a copy of the lease when a sale is contemplated.

In the Land Registry are details of each property giving all information in three sections; the property register, the ownership register and the charges on the property. On payment of a fee an owner or anyone having written consent, can obtain a copy of entries on the register.

The details maintained on the register include whether the property is freehold or leasehold with a description of its identity and address with reference to a plan showing the house or flat involved usually coloured for easy identification. Where a lease is involved there will be a description of the type of lease, the ground rent payable and to whom. Ownership is stipulated under the heading Proprietorship Register. There will be the words 'title absolute'. That indicates that the person whose name is given is guaranteed as the unchallengeable owner. There will also be stated the price paid for the property though this is not disclosed before a proposed sale to a new purchaser. As successive purchases are made, previous owners are struck out. The last part of the register, dealing with charges, gives details of mortgages or covenants.

While anyone can discover from the Land Registry whether or not a property is registered, and its title number, other details are barred unless a person has permission from the registered owner.

In sales there is a Land Registry fee to be paid which depends upon the price of the property involved, and is met by the purchaser. See Table 6 on page 133.

Lands Tribunal   One of several tribunals established to consider disputes. The Lands Tribunal deals among other things with disputes over valuation of properties affected by compulsory purchase orders and there are legal aid facilities where these are warranted. Where a landowner and a leaseholder do not agree there can be an appeal to the Lands Tribunal, which in fact is an informal court. It is composed of a number of chartered surveyors and barristers. There is also provision for appeals to the Tribunal where there is a dispute over rates assessments.

Law Society   Solicitors' professional organization which maintains a register of members, has a code of conduct to which they conform and which will deal with complaints about them from the public.

Leasehold   A leasehold is a form of tenancy under which a ground rent is paid to the freehold owner of land or buildings for a specific number of years. Building leases are usually granted for 99 or 999 years; other leases, for houses or flats, are usually for terms between 21 and 99 or 999 years, though in the case of flats leases are often granted for much shorter periods. In the case of a repairing lease, a tenant, or lessee as he is called, is required to keep the premises he leases in a sound state of repair. At the end of the term of a lease the land and buildings on it became the property of the ground landlord, the freeholder, or his successors and a requirement was that the property must be handed over in good repair.

Today the leaseholder of a house (not a flat) has more protection;

under the provisions of the Leasehold Reform Act, 1967, he is able either to purchase the freehold or to extend the term of the lease at a new negotiated ground rent, provided that he has lived in the property for at least five years (or for five out of the last ten years), that the lease was originally granted for more than 21 years at a low rent and that the property falls within prescribed rateable value limits.

Some builders offer homes on a leasehold basis more cheaply than if they are freehold, the former fixing a ground rent which shows them a return on the value of the site on which the houses stand. Usually in such cases, the leaseholder is able to negotiate the acquisition of the freehold at any time during the period of the lease.

An existing property subject to a lease will vary in price depending upon how long the lease has to run. Building societies are reluctant to advance loans on leaseholds under 60 years. Leases stipulate certain conditions such as how often the exterior of a house should be painted and that it should be kept in good repair. Repairs must not be undertaken without the landlord's consent. Leasehold properties can be used only for the purposes laid down in the lease, thus a house may only be used residentially and not for business.

Flats are leaseholds generally so that there is a collective responsibility for common parts, such as corridors, staircases, roofs and the gardens, and there will be a service charge to pay for things like porterage, constant hot water and central heating and the patrolling of corridors and so on.

There will be variations in a lease which relates to a flat which has been constructed from a former single house. In a number of cases, such flats are above the ground-floor unit often occupied by the owner of the house. It is general for the occupant of the top-floor flat to be responsible for the good state of the roof and for the ground-floor occupant to take on responsibility for the drains and other surface services.

It is common these days for those in flats in large blocks to form residents' associations or management associations which levy fees on all occupants equally for the upkeep of the building. Building societies are less inclined to advance a loan on flats which are sold as freeholds with a residents' committee appointed to supervise maintenance and repairs than on leaseholds where the responsibility for communal ownership is clearly set out.

Lessee A leaseholder to whom an original lease was granted; one who holds a lease. He has as lessee a legal right in a property for a fixed term of years so long as he meets the conditions of his lease, the main one of which is the payment of a ground rent for the property. A lease is granted by a lessor.

Lessor He must, if a lease is granted for more than three years, execute a deed which names and describes the parties to the lease and the terms on which it is granted. These terms may include a wide variety and should be carefully scrutinized. Normally they cover such matters as keeping the property in good repair, maintaining insurance on it, decorating inside and outside at stated intervals and possibly carrying out certain repairs. It is customary for the original of the lease to be 'signed, sealed and delivered' by the lessor and conveyed to the lessee which is evidence of his title to the property; the lessee also performs the signing and sealing and handing over a copy to the lessor as acceptance of the terms and conditions in the lease.

Letting your home If an owner is not able to live in his house himself for a time he may wish to let it to someone else. Into this category fall retired couples who buy a bungalow or country cottage in advance of finishing employment and others who owning a house, are obliged to go abroad for a few years. These involve not only Service personnel who are today quite prominent among owners but also employees of multi-national firms who move their staffs around from country to country for a term of duty.

One thing is certain; any letting must be made on the basis of a very tightly-worded agreement under which an undertaking is given by a tenant to return the property to its owner when it is required. Even so it is far from plain sailing always to have a property and its owner reunited.

Many absent owners have found that the easiest way is to let their homes to a Government agency or to a foreigner working in this country. Neither is affected by the various Rent Acts which protect tenants in the ordinary way. Experience has shown that even when an owner has right on his side the courts are reluctant to find in his favour without providing some safeguard, usually an extension of tenure, for the tenant.

In practice that means that owners should start proceedings, if necessary, for a return of their properties well in advance of the date they actually require them. There is a leaflet issued by the Department of the Environment on the subject of how to get one's home back if it has been let on a temporary basis but it is quick to point out that it is not an authoritative explanation of the law and that those considering letting their homes are advised to consult a solicitor for advice appropriate to their individual circumstances.

The leaflet in no way replaces the various Rent Acts on which the whole question is hinged. Under the Acts, courts must grant an order for possession to temporarily-absent owners returning home and to people retiring 'subject to certain procedures' being followed. There are explanations of the procedures in the leaflet and their compliance so that owners who rent out their homes are able to gain possession when they require the accommodation.

Conditions which must be observed include that under which if an owner lets his property, furnished or unfurnished, he should give the tenant written notice, at or before the time the tenancy is granted, hat possession of the property is to be recovered.

Each time a new tenancy is created such written notice must be given. That is the only way to be *certain* that a court order will be granted.

Where an owner acquired a home with a view to occupying it on retirement and let it on a protected tenancy a court must grant a repossession order if, not later than the beginning of any tenancy the owner gave written notice of his intention and the court is satisfied that the owner has retired from full-time employment and requires the property as his home. There is also provision for repossession when an owner has died and a member of his family who was living with him at the time of his death needs the dwelling for a home.

The leaflet, along with further advice, is obtainable from rent officers, council offices, citizens' advice bureaux or housing aid centres. It is called 'Letting your own home' and is free. It is however sound advice to put the whole matter of letting temporarily in the hands of a competent estate agent who will look after the property in the absence of an owner and collect the rent. He will also see to any necessary repairs and will attend to the legal aspects of the situation if necessary.

He will also make sure that gardens are properly cared for, and, if the house is furnished, that breakages are replaced by the tenant. Leaving such matters to the goodwill or whim of the temporary occupant is a dicey procedure and it is better to have strict adherence to the rules emphasized through a third party on the spot.

Several agents will advise against letting properties for set terms to individual families and will rather seek foreign Government tenants. Agreements are then made with the Governments concerned which undertake to vacate the premises when they are required. It is then up to those agencies to find alternative accommodation for their officials' families and they will rarely take the matter to a court. Court proceedings can be dragged out to such an extent that the whole object of an owner's having bought a home in advance of his immediate requirements is lost.

On a more general theme, renting out vacant accommodation is no longer the plain-sailing operation it used to be. Successive governments have introduced legislation over the years to control the whole business of renting, and small, as well as large landlords are subject to it.

The 1974 Rent Act, brought in by the Labour administration, is considered by landlords to be the harshest yet. Under it, both furnished and unfurnished accommodation is covered, with the net result that the supply of rented homes is drying up as landlords decide its maintenance is not worth the bother and expense involved for the returns possible under rent controls. Paradoxically every piece of legislation which has been introduced ostensibly to protect tenants has worked against them in the long run as property owners have steadily dispensed with accommodation which otherwise they would have let.

A valuable and additional source of rented accommodation traditionally was that of the couple who bought, for example, a country or seaside property in anticipation of living there permanently a few years hence who, as stated above, are now caught up in the Rent Acts' provisions.

It is because such properties acquired for eventual retirement though excluded from the provisions of the 1974 Rent Act are affected by other protective legislation that complications can arise. The point is that, under the law as it stands, individuals landlords and tenants are not permitted to agree any enforceable terms for a long tenancy.

There was the case of a clergyman who, within a few years of retirement, bought a bungalow at Torquay which he let to a family meantime. When about to give up his vicarage he found the tenants adamant that they would not leave on the grounds that the family had nowhere to go. That was despite a written promise to vacate the bungalow when it was required by the clergyman and his wife (who incidentally had been obliged to vacate their vicarage to the next incumbent). Recourse was had to the court, the clergyman arguing that his need of the bungalow was not only necessary but urgent. The court granted the tenants two months and then a further two months to find alternative accommodation. Meanwhile the clergyman and his wife had four months' costly hotel bills.

Quite apart from the problems associated with obtaining possession tenants have opportunities to seek revisions of rents, downwards of course, if they feel these have been set too high.

In fact rents are controlled in that manner so that an owner is unlikely to get a fair return on his capital, more so when taxation is taken into account. If a small bungalow, say, valued at £12,000, is let, the rent should be at least £25 to £50 a week, depending upon whether or not it is furnished, but an appeal against those levels would certainly be upheld by a rent officer. Usually the level for such accommodation is £10 to £15 a week which shows a very poor return on the investment involved.

Faced with a battery of complicated legal machinery, agents advise owners wishing to recover properties to start proceedings at least a year in advance. In that way the courts' penchant for giving tenants lengthy intervals in which to find alternative accommodation can usually be covered.

Building societies are very chary of giving consent to let a house being bought with the aid of a loan. Should a borrower fail to maintain his mortgage repayments and the society wish to possess the property it may have to allow any tenant to remain permanently even though the borrower departs. Where a building society borrower wishes to sublet, furnished, part of his home consent from the lending body must be sought and in fact is usually given.

Some owners, particularly the more elderly, who occupy houses or flats too large for their present needs and who would like income and possibly, company, from a tenant, might equally find themselves trapped by current legislation. It used to be the practice to let off spare rooms or floors providing the letting was furnished but many have now decided to discontinue this as the risks are considered too great and the return by way of rent too restrictive.

Actually, in the case of 'resident landlords' there is exemption from the Rent Acts but there are technical considerations which must be safeguarded against. Flats in a landlord's premises must be separated one above the other and there are problems about separate accomodation otherwise provided, say adjacent to the main house, and an argument could well result in a court hearing. Courts too, are brought into the picture where tenants might turn out to be undesirable, not only by failure to pay their rents or because they are socially objectionable, but also for any other cause.

A new form of tenancy, was introduced under the Housing Act 1980. Called 'shorthold' tenancies, they allow for letting at 'fair' rents for fixed terms of between one and five years. The tenant has full security of tenure for the term of the lease but the landlord has the right to regain possession at the end of the term.

Licence to assign A clause in a lease stipulates that a leaseholder is required to obtain the consent of the landlord should he wish to assign the lease to another person. The landlord's agreement to this is known as the licence to assign.

Life insurance Many home-buyers take the precaution of taking out insurance in cases where they have committed themselves to a high mortgage over a long term. The usual method is to take out insurance which covers at least half of the total amount of a building society mortgage; if a loan has been granted by an assurance company, the insurance cover will be for the full amount of the mortgage. There are special mortgage protection policies where borrowing has been made in other circumstances.

Lighting A quick study will soon establish whether or not lights are correctly or badly placed and if they are not providing illumination where it is most wanted then something should be done about it. Those not capable of handling new electrical installations, and that goes for most of us, should certainly have any extensions or installations attended to by an electrician. It is highly dangerous not only to tamper but also to have long lengths of wire trailing about floors or benches. All electrical leads should be kept as short as possible which presupposes a generous supply of sockets and plugs, and of the correct load-bearing capacities.

Listed buildings Purchasers should take care about acquiring a 'listed building', that is a building which has been noted by a local authority as being worthy of preservation due to its historic or architectural interests. These buildings carry official protection from alteration or demolition except by explicit permission. Such listed properties can be expensive to maintain and repair because of the specialist nature of their construction and age so that it is as well for the prospective buyer to know what is being taken on by their purchase.

Almost all houses which qualify for the adjective 'period' come into the category of listed and that usually includes everything built before the Victorian era. Even then, some early Victorian houses of note are listed where they have special attributes, particularly if they have been built in Georgian or Regency style. Local authorities keep note of listed buildings and it is a wise precaution to inquire where there might be any doubt whether a property is on the list or not. Lists are continually being added to and there is a quip in the property world that some officials brand as period and therefore worth listing, any house which is older than themselves! That of course is a wild exaggeration but as the years pass additional properties do come up for consideration and inclusion.

At the same time, local councils are very much concerned to keep in good repair the accredited period properties in their areas and it is always a good point to remember to ask if there is any way that owners can be helped with the cost of repairs. For the largest houses with much historical and architectural interest the Historic Buildings Council is able to recommend grants for essential work.

Another point to watch is when a house is in a conservation area which usually is a street or part of a street, a square or other compact area designated again as worthy of preservation by a local authority. In such instances, while a building may not be 'listed' it does come within the purview of the Town and Country Amenities Act, 1974. Under that Act permission is required for the demolition of a building in a conservation area but is more than likely to be refused because the building is considered worth preserving (in the eyes of the authorities, that is!).

Loans Home-owners who wish to make improvements to old houses are sometimes eligible for loans from the local authority in whose territory the property involved stands. Applications for loans are considered on their merits by the local council and are usually made in connection with a grant which might be payable where certain basic amenities are being installed. Banks issue bridging loans for owners who, in the process of selling one house and buying another, require to be able to call on funds to meet expenses while the transaction is going through. Such loans are given on the understanding that they will be repaid when the deal is completed. Interest is charged at the rate in operation during the period of the loan.

Local search A special form sent to a local council asking for a certificate which gives certain information about a property in its area. It is used to ensure that a purchaser has no obstacles to buying of which he is unaware. These could include compulsory purchase orders or demolition orders or such like. Usually there is an accompanying form which provides additional information on proposals which might affect a particular property.

LVA (Land Valuation Act) form When a transaction for purchasing a home is completed the Inland Revenue expects to be told about it. Details of the acquisition are given on the LVA form, obtainable from Inland Revenue stamp offices or head post offices.

M

Maintenance Home-owners have a vital role to play when it comes to proper maintenance of their properties and vigilance can save money. Systematic inspections should be undertaken and visual faults rectified. Guttering should be cleared of leaves in the autumn, for example, and any stoppages cleared so that downcomers do not get clogged. Out-of-place tiles and slates can be spotted and fastened; badly-fitting doors and windows should be attended to. For substantial maintenance and repair, such as a roof requiring major attention and possibly replacing, a building society will sometimes provide the funds as an extension to an existing mortgage. Painting and decorating should be undertaken at regular intervals to preserve the fabric as well as to make the house look attractive. Gates and fences should not be overlooked; these can be expensive to replace if they are neglected.

Maisonette Accommodation occupying more than one floor, but unlike a flat, with a separate outside entrance though only forming part of a building. Like flats, maisonettes are usually sold on a leasehold basis.

Metric system Building construction now uses the metric system. Timber measurements are in metres and centimetres (100 to the metre) and areas are measured in hectares, equivalent to 100 ares. A hectare is about $2\frac{1}{2}$ acres (2·471 to be precise). Homes are beginning to be quoted in square metres (m^2) rather than square feet.

Mobile home Not as mobile really, as its name implies. A mobile home is a prefabricated, fully-furnished building which is mobile insofar as it is transported bodily on a trailer from manufacturer or supplier to a prepared site, there to be connected to main services.

Once on a site, a mobile home is rarely moved; indeed most people having them then add bits on to them such as verandas and porches, lean-to greenhouses and sheds. The homes are built on caravan principles and commonly referred to by their owners as 'vans'. It is normal for special parks to be set up to accommodate mobile homes, sites being leasehold and subject to supervision.

Attractions are immediately apparent to young couples or elderly single or retired people. A disadvantage so far as the young are concerned is that purchasing must be over a maximum of 10 years against up to 35 years for a mortgage on a house, though prices are very much lower than for the latter. Mobile homes, depending on size and finish, may be bought from about £3,000 to £9,000. All are after assembly, ready to be connected to main services, drains, water, electricity and gas if available. Prices usually include furnishings, central heating and very often a refrigerator. These instant homes however, are restricted in width in that to comply with road regulations for low-loader transporters on which they are carried, none must be wider than 10½ feet. Lengths can be anything up to 45 feet.

As far as accommodation is concerned, each mobile home contains two bedrooms and a living area, in bungalow style. Larger homes are provided by combining two or more smaller units to give at least double the space, so it is possible to have three or four bedrooms.

Some of the items installed are subject to value added tax and £200 or so invariably covers connections to services. With transport say, of 50 miles or so from dealer to site, between £500 and £600 additional to the purchase price should be budgeted for. Having a mobile home in fact means possession of a soundly constructed piece of equipment. They are made in aluminium, glass fibre and hardboard, highly and skilfully insulated and fully weather-protected and as such they are relatively inexpensive to heat. Regular normal maintenance is not more than an annual washdown and possibly, an occasional bit of painting, attention to guttering and so on.

Those who prefer it can site a mobile home on one of the 2,000 residential parks situated throughout the country; most of them in the southern half. Such parks are privately-operated and home-owners pay rents for their sites in them, which vary according to amenities provided. Anything from £3 to £6 a week should be estimated for but circumstances can alter things quickly, such as drastic falls in money values and increasing costs for site maintenance. Sites can accommodate any number from half a dozen homes to more than 200 and there is a shortage, which according to the overseeing body, the National Caravan Council, is due to the scarcity of planning consents for establishing new parks.

Rates are payable by mobile-home owners in the same way as other householders, to the local authority in whose area they reside. Providing parks are developed in a proper manner local councils are not averse to them. Indeed there is an obligation on local authorities, once a planning permission has been authorized, to grant a licence which lays down terms and conditions for its operation.

It is normal practice for a prospective buyer of a mobile home to approach the dealer from whom he will buy for details of available sites. Most dealers maintain lists of plots which have become vacant or are about to become vacant in the near future.

There are safeguards for mobile-home residents as well as for site operators under two Acts of Parliament. Occupiers of mobile homes on 'protected sites' are covered by the Caravan Sites Act of 1968. They are those who have hired a pitch or mobile home under a 'residential contract', an agreement under which a person is entitled to station a mobile home on a protected site and occupy it as his residence. The 1968 Act makes harassment an offence.

A later enactment is the Mobile Homes Act 1975 which broadly adds to the protection afforded by the earlier legislation. It applies to people who are renting pitches for their own mobile homes, not to those who rent a mobile home together with a plot. Under the Act owners of mobile-home sites must offer a written agreement to each resident who has stationed his mobile home on the site and who occupies it as his only main residence. Normally the agreement is for five years minimum with the option for the resident to renew it for a further three years, ensuring that where a resident does not wish to move he can count on an effective stay of eight years at least. The only exceptions are where a site owner's interest in the land or the planning permission for the use of the land as a mobile-home site, is due to run out in under that period.

Other benefits bestowed by the Act include the right of owners of mobile homes to sell them on site, subject to certain conditions. The Act does not prevent site owners and residents from including additional terms and conditions providing always that they do not conflict with the requirements of the legislation. Since October 1975, prospective residents must be offered an agreement before taking up occupation. In the event of a disagreement between site owner and resident on the terms of an agreement there is provision in the Act for terms to be settled by the courts. Provision is also made for succession rights for both site operator and mobile-home owner. Thus, for example, widows of either are protected. Under the agreements offered to mobile-home owners must be undertakings by the site operators about rents and by occupiers as to repairs to and maintenance of homes. Site owners can insist on 'reasonable standards' being maintained though there is nothing specific to indicate that mobile homes should be renewed at stated periods. Mobile-home owners have the same protection under other Acts as for other householders who seek relief from disturbance by neighbours and antisocial behaviour. Some information organizations include the Mobile Home Residents Association and the bi-monthly *Mobile Home*, the National Federation of Site Operators and the National Caravan Council.

Household names in mobile homes include Bluebird, Davan, Lisset and Omar. A unique site is offered by Marina Services (Medway) where a 'marina landhome' is available in the firm's residential park at Hoo, near Rochester, Kent. Country parks are operated in Yorkshire by Glen Parks and in Kent, too at Shirkoak Park, Woodchurch, 15 minutes from the coast. Other parks by the same operator are at Basingstoke, Chesham, Hemel Hempstead, Maidenhead and Slough.

Several residential parks are under the Godfrey Davis banner including that at Turners Hill, near Crawley, Sussex. Information may be obtained about others from sales centres in Epping, Egham, Coulsdon, Waltham Cross and Warninglid.

Mortgage Amounts advanced by way of mortgages are geared to the monthly repayments which a borrower can meet. Broadly mortgages are limited to $2\frac{1}{2}$ to three times the annual income of the applicant for a loan on the basis that monthly repayments should not exceed a week's wage or salary. It is possible that some societies will take into account the earnings of a wife and regular overtime and bonuses. Count on advances being made of not more than 80 per cent of the valuation of a property assessed by a building society surveyor. This will not necessarily be the same as the price quoted for a house or flat and is frequently lower. All societies wish to do is to ensure that their loan is well protected should they have to dispose of the property in the event of a mortgagor not being able to continue repayments. Societies will 'top up' their 80 per cent advances to 90 per cent or even 95 per cent by a once-for-all assurance premium which is normally added to the repayment arrangements and is seldom more than an additional £1.50 for a medium-size home.

There are various mortgage schemes – a straight repayment plan under which monthly repayments are made covering part of the capital and interest until the total is repaid; an endowment scheme under which, along with the amount borrowed, a borrower takes out an insurance policy to cover the capital, either with profits or without profits at the end of the term; and a low-cost scheme which is a variation of the with-profit endowment insurance plan under which insurance is taken out for a sum smaller than the capital involved in the house-purchase on the assumption that the policy will earn sufficient bonuses over the years to repay the loan in full at the end of the period for which the mortgage is granted.

Though the majority of mortgages are granted by building societies, life assurance companies will sometimes themselves grant a mortgage along with an endowment insurance policy. Local authorities have power to give mortgages though they only usually step in when an applicant has been unable to find another source. There are private funds also available from time to time for mortgage purposes; these are usually traceable through a solicitor or accountant and some finance houses also grant mortgages though at a flat rate of interest. Banks will give a mortgage generally only when a small portion of the purchase price has to be found in that way, say 20 per cent, and they would normally expect to see it paid off in five years.

In the purchase of new homes there are often mortgage advances to be obtained through the builder. Many building societies specifically allocate funds to building firms for the express purpose of assisting would-be purchasers to buy their homes. Other mortgages from other building societies of course are available too, should a buyer not wish to take advantage of those which have earmarked funds to a builder. Broadly the same conditions apply.

Mortgage broker On occasion, a mortgage broker will seek out a building society or insurance company ready to provide a loan for home-purchasing. Many estate agents use mortgage brokers to advantage in this way. A number of estate agents maintain what in effect is a mortgage broking department and will arrange loans for potential house-buyers. A mortgage broker should derive his fee from the side with whom he places the business; not from the applicant. Deal with mortgage brokers who are members of their professional body and so operate within a code of conduct.

Mortgage protection policy An insurance taken out specifically by a mortgagor to pay off the amount of a loan should he die before the end of the term for which the advance has been made. The premium payable for a policy of this nature depends upon the age of the mortgagor and the size of the loan but count on about £25 a year.

Mortgagee The lender of money on mortgage; a building society, assurance company, local authority, bank, finance house or private individual which has advanced funds on the security of the property being acquired.

Mortgagor The borrower of money on mortgage.

Moving on Estimates indicate that very few people buying a house remain in it for the full term of any mortgage they may have taken out. Moves on average are made every seven years (in some areas every five years), so it is likely that anyone with a loan will be faced not only with redeeming it but of taking out another. On a move a building society will ask for a loan to be repaid even though it is contemplated that another house will be bought with the aid of a further mortgage. Generally some of the capital will have been paid off so that the repayment to a society will be less than the amount of the original loan, but the size of any new loan will generally be larger and will be for a different number of years (or one or the other). This procedure also involves adjustment of insurance though if an existing loan is being repaid by schemes under the endowment or low-cost mortgage plans, the money earned may be used to help out by way of collateral security and the policies can be transferred to cover any new loan. If the new loan is higher than the amount covered by the policy and bonuses a new policy can be taken out to match the balance.

In addition to the various legal costs involved, what must not be forgotten are the actual costs of the move – the payment for removal men, items connected with electrical and gas installations, telephone, television, carpets, and curtains which normally must be replaced simply because those which fitted in the house vacated seldom are suitable for the home being moved into. Some of the costs may be small in themselves, but nevertheless in total add up to a tidy sum. The cost of a removal itself of course, depends upon the numbers of hours and men needed to load and unload the furniture and the size of the van booked along with the distance it and its personnel are required to travel. As a guide to costs, the tables below indicate what a seller/buyer may expect to budget for. Stamp duty starts above £20,000, from £20,001 to £25,000 the rate is $\frac{1}{2}$ per cent, from £25,001 to £30,000 the rate is 1 per cent; from £30,001 to £35,000 it is $1\frac{1}{2}$ per cent and £35,001 and over it is 2 per cent. When a new lease is granted stamp duty is set by the ground rent and not the purchase price.

TABLE 5

SELLING A HOUSE

House price £	Approximate Solicitors' fee* £	Approximate estate agents' fee† £
9,000	90	180
10,000	100	200
14,000	140	280
16,000	160	320
20,000	200	400
25,000	250	500
30,000	300	600
35,000	350	700
40,000	400	800

*There are no scale fees for solicitors, but generally the fees for the work in selling a house are generally pitched between $\frac{1}{2}$ per cent and 1 per cent of the sale price. The fee may be at a higher percentage for lower-priced houses than for higher-valued property

†Estate agents' commissions are generally pitched between $1\frac{1}{2}$ and 3 per cent of the price realized on a sale although they are negotiable and should be agreed in advance. In Scotland solicitors acting as agents have a maximum scale fee of $1\frac{1}{2}$ per cent.

TABLE 6

BUYING A HOUSE

Price £	Stamp duty £	Land Registry fee* £	Building society survey fees† £	Independent valuation fee £
9,000	nil	22·50	19	52·50
10,000	nil	25	21	57·50
12,000	nil	30	25	67·50
14,000	nil	35	29	73·75
16,000	nil	40	32	78·75
18,000	nil	45	34	83·75
20,000	nil	50	36	88·75
25,000	125	62·50	41	101·25
30,000	300	75	46	113·75
35,000	525	87·50	49	126·25
40,000	800	100	51	138·75

*Land Registry fees are approximately ¼ per cent of the price.
†Building Society fees are to a scale of fees based on the total price and include VAT.

Scale fees for solicitors ended in 1972 and no longer apply for estate agents' commissions and therefore should be agreed in advance.

TABLE 7

MOVING THE FURNITURE

Distance miles		Three-bedroom semi £	Two-bedroom flat £
100 to 150	say	190	180
200 to 250		330	320

Subject to VAT

Note: Much depends upon the time factor. A flat on the top floors of a block will obviously take longer to deal with than a ground-floor unit. Some items may have to be lowered through windows. Similarly, a house having a long front garden will take longer to clear than one straight on to the road. Cumbersome furniture and delicate items which require special handling will also have to be taken into account. Estimates should be obtained from several removers. Sometimes small loads can be accommodated with another move in the same direction; also often it is possible for a remover to fit in a return load thus cutting down his overall costs with benefit to the house-owner.

TABLE 8

COST OF BUILDING SOCIETY
INTEREST AND PRINCIPAL

for each £1,000	years	$11\frac{1}{2}\%$ £	12% £	$12\frac{1}{2}\%$ £	13% £	$13\frac{1}{2}\%$ £	14% £	$14\frac{1}{2}\%$ £
	1	92·92	93·34	93·76	94·18	94·60	95·02	95·44
	2	48·99	49·31	49·64	49·96	50·28	50·59	50·91
	3	34·40	34·70	35·00	35·30	35·60	35·90	36·20
	5	22·84	23·12	23·41	33·69	23·97	24·25	24·53
	10	14·45	14·75	15·06	15·36	15·66	15·97	16·27
	15	11·92	12·24	12·57	12·90	13·23	13·56	13·89
	20	10·81	11·16	11·51	11·86	12·21	12·56	12·91
	25	10·26	10·63	11·00	11·37	11·74	12·11	12·48
	30	9·97	10·35	10·74	11·12	11·50	11·88	12·26

TABLE 9

CALENDAR MONTHLY INSTALMENTS TO REPAY A LOAN OF £1,000
FROM A BUILDING SOCIETY

Years	11%	12%	13%	13½%	14%	14½%	15%
5	22·55	23·12	23·70	22·99	24·28	24·57	24·86
10	14·16	14·75	15·36	15·67	15·98	16·29	16·61
15	11·59	12·24	12·90	13·23	13·57	13·91	14·26
20	10·47	11·16	11·87	12·23	12·59	12·95	13·32
25	9·90	10·63	11·37	11·75	12·13	12·51	12·90
30	9·59	10·35	11·12·	11·51	11·91	12·30	12·70

These are the gross payments per month. Income Tax relief is not given on
mortgages above £25,000.

N

National House-Building Council The body which was originally
established as the National House-Builders Registration Council which
undertook to introduce a register of recognized and accepted house-
builders. Houses of a builder registered by the council are inspected
periodically during the course of construction. Building is to defined
quality standards and there is an after-sales guarantee with provision
for a buyer to be insured against major defects. In cases of dispute
between a builder and purchaser, there is a means of arbitration to settle
any issue.

Building societies insist that newly-built houses for which mortgages
are granted should have been erected by a builder who is a member of
the Council and is in a position to give the 10-year guarantee with after-
sales service. There are exceptions in cases where a house has been built
under the supervision of an architect or qualified surveyor employed by
the buyer.

Advantages of dealing with registered builders and developers include
the acceptance by firms that they will at least comply with minimum
standards laid down in the Council's requirements, allow inspections
of their work, will provide a two-year warranty against defects

and a 10-year protection against major structural faults.

No one pretends that the inspection process is foolproof but what is important is that the registered house-builder has agreed to a set of rules and it is up to a purchaser's solicitor (or himself) to see that the agreement in fact is entered into.

The agreement is a legal document which binds the builder to remedy at his own expense any defects which may arise as a result of his failure to comply with the Council's specification for standards of workmanship and materials. A provision is that a buyer must notify the builder in writing reasonably soon after the defect has occurred and within two years of the Council's certificate. The agreement covers defects only, not normal wear and tear or normal shrinkage. Central heating boilers and electrical moving parts are covered for one year.

Once a house is certified the Council, subject to certain limitations, will honour any arbitration award which may ensue and which a builder might not pay. Between the third and tenth year major defects in the load-bearing structure of a house are also protected under insurance arrangements with the Council. Those dealing with firms which become bankrupt or go into liquidation are covered by the Council's guarantees to purchasers.

The Council stresses that purchasers of new homes should know what they are buying. As far as specification is concerned, the minimum requirements if adhered to, will produce a sound well-built house, but they do not cover fitments or extras which may be ordered by purchasers. Builder and buyer should agree in advance, where choice of equipment and so on, is concerned, that is, for decorations, colour schemes and the rest. In the interests both of the buyer and builder the Council recommends that a pre-entry inspection be made to ascertain the condition of glass, sanitary ware, other breakables and that any special facets have been complied with. If hidden defects later emerge the Council points out that this will not prevent the purchaser's seeking redress under the NH-BC agreement. On the other hand the time to report cracked glass, chipped baths or washbasins and that sort of thing is at the time of entry and not two months later! At that stage it would be difficult for anyone to establish who caused the damage.

All new properties suffer a certain amount of shrinkage. Consider the amount of water used during their construction; some 1,500 gallons, it is estimated have been absorbed by bricks, timbers and other materials. As houses are lived in they dry out and wood and plaster, in particular, shrink. The small cracks which appear are not structurally important and may be sealed in the ordinary course of events by normal redecoration. Unless the cracks are abnormally large the builder is not committed to putting them right. Though most builders take precautions over allowing materials to get wet during bad weather, there is always some absorption from the atmosphere. Owners of new homes are therefore advised to 'run them in' just as carefully as they would a new car. The great thing is never to turn on heating at full blast; allow a house to warm up slowly and naturally, giving it plenty ventilation. Failure to do this can result in condensation and in bad cases, a mould on plaster and woodwork. The key is always to be certain that ventilation is proper and adequate.

A sign of drying out is a white deposit which sometimes appears on walls, both inside and out. It is called efflorescence and is not serious needing no more than a swift wipe off if the deposits, which are salts, are unsightly.

It may be some time, because of legalities, before a builder can hand over the NH-BC certificate and buyers should insist that a clause covering the point is inserted in the agreement to purchase.

In periods of recession many firms go out of business and their names are removed from the NH-BC register. As a result firms are unable to sell or to contract to build any more houses carrying the Council's 10-year protection. Receivers appointed to act in cases where builders or developers have gone into liquidation are entitled to apply to be added to the register as developers or builders. Receivers then have to enter into the NH-BC house-purchaser's agreement for all dwellings sold. Should a receiver wish to register as a builder he must employ the management of the original building firm with the approval of the Council. In this way the buyer is able to obtain a certificate for a property and thus qualify to obtain his mortgage.

Neighbours   It is said and it is true, that to have good neighbours one must be a good neighbour oneself. That borrowed lawnmower must, in law, be returned when the lender asks for it but it is better to return it before he does! Good neighbours invariably hold keys to one another's homes so that they can keep an eye on things in emergencies and absences. Neighbours have rights in law to object to proposed extensions to properties which might make their own homes less attractive both from the point of living in them and in the event of having to sell them. Any householder who considers he has an objection to a neighbour's proposals is able to write to his local authority and lodge an official complaint. There are powers for him to take his objection as high as the Minister of Housing if necessary. Boundaries between houses are sometimes not readily defined in title deeds and owners in dispute may decide to settle the matter in court.

Noise   Much unpleasantness between neighbours is caused through noise. Flat-dwellers are particularly prone to this irritation as many walls and floors are insufficiently insulated. In very bad cases of noise by neighbours a court order is the only solution though three or more neighbours may complain to the local authority which is empowered to take steps to prevent it. Raw notes struck on a musical instrument may be considered noise but it is unlikely that anyone would or could take steps to stop them unless they were being deliberately and unreasonably played at an ungodly hour specially to annoy.

Norman A form of architecture recognizable by rounded arches; seen in some of the country's oldest buildings dating from the Norman Conquest in 1066.

Notary Usually a solicitor who attests and certifies documents. In purchases of properties abroad, a notary handles the final transactions on behalf of both parties, for which he receives a fee. He is not employed either by the seller or the purchaser but is an official appointed by the authorities.

Nuisance Some annoyances fall into the category of being nuisances and there is a law to deal with them. A court can make an order against a neighbour who it can be proved, is interfering with a person's comfort and convenience by acting unreasonably. A complainant may be able to obtain an injunction to stop the neighbour so conducting himself and there might be a case for damages though that would be unlikely unless there was persistence over a period particularly if evil-smelling fumes are involved.

O

Option mortgage Where a person purchasing a home is not obtaining income tax relief it is to his advantage to take out an option mortgage. The yearly repayments in fact are higher than those incurred under an ordinary mortgage taking tax relief at maximum rates into account, but of course the capital sum is paid off more rapidly. The value of the ordinary mortgage decreases as far as tax is concerned as the capital is repaid.

Overriding interest These are rights which are enforceable against a property. They may not be entered on the register of the property at the Land Registry but nevertheless are applicable. The commonest example would be where a tenant of a house was to remain in possession after its sale despite the fact that his tenancy was not referred to on the register.

Overseas purchases Tackled the proper way, it is no more complicated to purchase overseas than it is at home. There are rules and regulations which must be complied with and, if that is done, then any transaction should be completed without any undue complications. A first essential is to decide where it is proposed a home abroad should be bought. To that end, it is wise to spend some time in the chosen locality, getting to know it in its various moods and also meeting local people, trying out the shopping and investigating the services. A long holiday is therefore indicated, and not by any means when the weather can be counted upon to be at its best. Money spent initially in this way can save much heartache later.

A reputable agent specializing in the sale of overseas property will be invaluable. He will provide a sheaf of brochures which will give a fair idea of the areas of which he has most knowledge. Be sure he has been to see the place and ask him details about it. Do *not* sign any document or pay any money over at any stage until you have enlisted a solicitor's expert knowledge, preferably one having experience of buying and selling overseas properties. He will tell you what and when to pay.

Exchange Control regulations have been scrapped, so it is no longer necessary to obtain the Bank of England's permission to transmit money overseas for home purchases, either when emigrating or buying a holiday home.

This relaxation has led to a number of ownership schemes which are described as 'timesharing', under which a property is acquired through a specialist company which offers to let your house or villa at times when you are not using it. Great care must be taken to ensure that the income from these lettings is sufficient to cover your commitments. Often the income is well below the cost of repayments, and buyers have found that statements and promises made by those selling the homes are not fulfilled.

Many estate agents who are operating abroad and who also have offices in this country, have endeavoured to protect potential buyers by having forms of contracts printed with the details of the properties they are selling. However, it is considered advisable to ensure that every contract is scrutinized by a professional, preferably one who can read it in the original language of the country in which the property involved is situated.

The fierce competition among the world's leading airlines over the past few years, which has resulted in fares to many places being dramatically reduced, has brought a far wider selection of locations for holiday homes within the reach, and pockets, of those seeking that foreign retreat. Many are now even searching in the sun belt of the United States for suitable houses for family holidays.

In the United States it is absolutely essential for a purchaser of any type of property to obtain the services of a lawyer. Such services are not cheap, even by British standards, but nonetheless necessary if buyers are to avoid unscrupulous sellers. The fixed rate, non-recourse mortgage which was once available in the United States is now unobtainable, and while some banks lend for house purchase, it is generally much more difficult to obtain loans there than it is in the United Kingdom.

Most buyers borrow locally if they can, but if this is not possible they take the cash with them from the United Kingdom. If you borrow locally and repay from the United Kingdom, you leave yourself open to losses on currency fluctuations, which can add a great deal to the cost.

While it is now possible to transfer all the sterling required for overseas purchase, potential buyers should look very carefully into the tax position, for they may find that there is a capital gains tax liability when they come to sell.

Buying procedures vary from country to country, though most Continental areas which Britons favour use the offices of a notary, who is a public official. It is customary in Italy, for example, for a buyer who has found the property he wishes to buy to be asked by the local agent to sign a *compromesso* or promissory contract. That will also be signed by the seller of the property. The *compromesso* may be sent to England for signature and at the time of signing the buyer will be expected to pay a third of the sale price to the seller. This should not be done without having ascertained that the procedure is in order. The final contract has to be signed by both parties or by those holding power of attorney. Signing is done before a notary to whom the full sale price, plus registration and notarial fees, has to be paid. Fees are about 9 per cent. As the notary is an official appointed by the authorities he is neither acting for buyer nor seller even though the purchaser has to meet his fees. There is also a *geometra*'s fee for drawing up the *compromesso* and final contract and for checking the documents involved. This comes to nearly 2 per cent of the sale price.

In France, a purchaser having found the property he wishes to own will be asked by the local agent to sign a *compromis* or *sous-seing privé* which similarly will be signed by the seller. There may be an application for a 10 per cent deposit at that stage. Again the final proceedings are in front of a notary to whom the full price of the property with the registration and notarial fees must be paid in advance. The buyer's fees are dependent upon the size of the property, worked out as a percentage of the sale price, and are normally between 10 and 5 per cent on a decreasing scale.

Now that more executives and technicians as well as holiday and retirement purchasers are concerned with purchasing properties abroad, particularly those going to jobs in countries forming the European Economic Community, fees payable are of more than passing interest. It is true to say that in general fees to be met by buyers for house-purchase are higher than those in Britain or Eire.

Several European agents charge both purchasers and sellers fees on a transaction whereas in the British Isles, unless a purchaser specifically appoints an agent to act on his behalf, he does not have to meet fees. These are paid by the vendor.

A common practice on the Continent is to levy 6 per cent of the cost of a house or flat being sold on the seller and 4 per cent on the buyer. These are exclusive of the various notary costs, Government taxes and duties and in some cases Value Added Tax on the total costs of a purchase. Building Societies do not exist in Continental countries and loans where available, are invariably issued through banks, many of which carry on departments for this very purpose. Interest rates vary a good deal too; in Spain a purchaser may obtain mortgages at about 10 per cent reducing.

Terms are not lengthy by British standards and seldom are loans outstanding for more than 15 years and more usually are limited to 5 or 10. Certainly in France, where interest on borrowings for house purchase is often 14 per cent or more, they would be for shorter periods than 15 years and they are normally subject to a small tax relief.

Unlike the United Kingdom, many other member countries of the European Economic Community have much property which can be rented and indeed landlords are encouraged officially to provide accommodation to let.

Intending purchasers abroad should be especially careful about taking over old properties. It is frequently the case that the title to such buildings is obscure and can be invested in several members of a family, some of whom may be far from easily traced, if indeed they can be found at all. Such properties as these can cause endless delays and lengthy and expensive complications and so are best avoided. As far as new developments are concerned, caution is again recommended. Agreements with builders and developers or their agents which might seem straightforward to the layman used only to British documents may be fraught with difficulties through clauses which in a lawyer's eyes would be unacceptable.

Recommendation is important when buying abroad just as it is in this country. Agents and solicitors who are well-known and have a long and honest history of the type of work involved, should be sought out and used. Most of them are only too willing to explain in detail and at length the procedures to be adopted and the pitfalls into which the unwary might be expected to drop. One can't be too careful nor ask too many questions. Better safe than sorry. Most agents and developers have facilities for flying out intending purchasers to view schemes and these should always be taken advantage of.

Reputable agents and developers, and there are many of them, prefer clients who investigate everything thoroughly. There is no mileage for them in a disgruntled or dissatisfied client as he is a bad advertisement not only for them but also for the developments with which they may be concerned.

There are certain general points which might profitably be borne in mind when contemplating living abroad. Most of the offices of governments abroad are represented in this country and have information departments from which a good deal of general guidance may be obtained. There will also be details of general conditions and climate, medical, scholastic and other services and, where applicable, whether or not there are arrangements to ensure that pensioners can receive their pensions and avoid paying income tax twice.

Some countries have reciprocal agreements under which pension increases granted in Britain are payable in those places. These include Austria, Belgium, Bermuda, Cyprus, Denmark, Finland, France, West Germany, Gibraltar, Eire, Israel, Italy, Jamaica, Jersey and Guernsey, Luxembourg, Malta, Netherlands, Spain, Switzerland, Turkey and Yugoslavia. To date increases are not paid in Australia, Canada, New Zealand and South Africa. Those who have emigrated and have left funds in this country may apply for them after having been domiciled elsewhere for four years. According to a Bank of England official, the applications are not normally rejected.

For details of medical treatment abroad, the Department of Health & Social Security has a leaflet on the subject which is supplied free. There are reciprocal arrangements with some countries and not others with the National Health Service and details may be obtained from the Overseas Group of the DHSS.

Owners' rights Along with many rights which owners have go obligations and responsibilities to others. The principle in law is that a man must exercise his rights over his own property without causing damage or nuisance to the property of his neighbours. Some things may be presumed; houses built in a row or semi-detached necessarily have the right of support of each other, so that pulling down or altering walls which rest against or are in other contact with adjoining property can be injurious. Similarly, where a neighbour's building is supported say by adjacent soil, removal of the soil would constitute an actionable deed. In flats occupants have the right to necessary support from walls and floors and ceilings, though they have the use of staircases, lifts and other means of access ownership of which is normally retained by the builder, developer or owning investment family or company.

When a man builds at the extreme edge of his land his neighbour is entitled to erect a wall or fence on his own land, even if the lights of building are obstructed. Vibration is classed as an annoyance and most owners suffer from it rather than have rights to it! These days serious defects can be caused to properties on roads which are incessantly used by heavily-laden juggernauts. Old properties which are close to road-sides are particularly prone to damage by vibrations caused in this way. There have been cases where compensation has been awarded for vibration. In one the owner of a house was successful where a court accepted his plea that his property had suffered due to pile-driving operations for a new building on the opposite side of the street.

While a dilapidated property is an eyesore an owner is under no obligation to a neighbour to keep his home in good repair or to paint it. Should a building deteriorate to the point where it becomes dangerous, an action could be brought or the local authority's building inspectorate could take appropriate remedial steps.

Trees which overhang or roots which penetrate a neighbour's plot may constitute a nuisance and branches which project thus may be cut without reference to the neighbour. Other items which have been placed on a person's land by a neighbour may also be removed. If trees overhang and obstruct a highway, the local authority can order the occupier of the land or house to have them cut back. Trees and fences which hinder views at corners and are considered to contribute to danger on roads, may be removed, though owners would be compensated for that.

P

Palladian Named after the Italian architect, Andrea Palladio, whose methods influenced Inigo Jones while studying in Venice. The latter introduced the Palladian style of architecture to this country and a number of substantial country houses designed by Inigo Jones bear the Italian influence. Noted for their proliferation of columns.

Part-use for business purposes While capital gains tax is not payable on a house or flat which is the main residence of the seller the tax is liable to be charged where a room or part of the property has been used for business purposes. Allowances are given to owners who set aside a room in their homes for business or professional work and when a sale takes place that room is treated separately as a taxable asset. The amount of tax liability depends upon what proportion of the whole, the room or other premises, say the garage, has been assessed as allowable for tax purposes.

Party walls These are walls separating adjoining homes, such as in terrace and semi-detached housing. They are considered to be owned vertically between the respective occupants. Each owner has the right of support and use. Where flats are concerned every wall and floor and ceiling may be party-owned.

Patio From the Spanish. In Spain it refers to an inner courtyard; in England it has come to be accepted as a paved area adjoining a house. Depending upon its size it is used for eating and sitting out, displaying plants and holding barbecues. Sometimes part of the patio is covered or enclosed to enable it to be used when the weather is less kind.

Penthouse Accommodation at the top of a block of flats is usually referred to as the penthouse or penthouse suite as it frequently absorbs more than one floor, unlike the units underneath. Many penthouses are lavishly equipped, often to the specific requirements of the person buying it. Some London penthouses are the most expensive styles of accommodation to be had and on two or three floors can have six or more bedrooms, six bathrooms, an entertaining level of considerable dimensions as well as ancillary domestic and kitchen quarters.

Period property This includes anything built up to early Victorian times. Some of the best examples of period architecture are seen in the country's largest houses, particularly those presiding over extensive estates. Unfortunately the biggest and most expensive to run of these houses have not been so popular because of rising costs and there is some consternation over what will eventually become of them.

Certain counties and regions produce the best choice of period houses; Essex, particularly close to the Suffolk border, has a variety of houses dating from the 14th century, much in timber-frame styling with others in Sussex and Kent of the cob-and-lath type. Shropshire is, with Cheshire, noted for 'black-and-white' architectural specimens, Worcestershire and Herefordshire, with other agrarian counties, have a quota of cottages of some antiquity.

Certain architectural styles are indistinguishable, being 'mergers' of several types. In a number of cases, houses of one period have been added to in other generations, either in similar fashion or in the fashion of the period during which the extensions were made. Thus a buyer is able to find say, a basically Elizabethan or Tudor house with Georgian additions, Georgian properties with Victorian extensions and so on. Several of the more recently-constructed 'period' homes are in fact, not period in the true sense but have been erected in period style using old materials obtained from buildings demolished.

Many of the period houses are manorial buildings, and the Elizabethan era produces numbers of this type, some of E-shape constructed around a courtyard. They are outstanding externally because of certain features, including octagonal chimneys in narrow brick. Tudor houses are often identified by the half-timbered elevations. In Scotland there are baronial 'castles' of some antiquity in the more choice rural situations, especially on the river banks where they do, or once did, preside over wide acres of woodlands and lochs.

Towns throw up a range between isolated 13th, 14th and 15th century cottages and lofty Georgian terraces. The fate of many of these terraces has been decided by economics. If London is taken as one example and Edinburgh as another, the only way to preserve the best of these expansive Georgian houses, once the town homes of the wealthy landowners, merchants and noblemen, has been to convert them into separate flats and maisonettes. Typical of the adaptations are those in London's Eaton Square and in Edinburgh's Moray Place. Even when individual flats are created in what were formerly large town houses, the units themselves are very extensive by modern standards and prices match both the standard of conversion and the convenience for owners in living close to the centres of large cities which cuts out both the cost and time of travelling. To a great extent the same thing has happened in towns and cities which were spas when it was fashionable to 'take the waters' and large houses were built by followers of the Royal households of the time. The larger period houses in Harrogate and Cheltenham are examples of this.

Elizabethan and Tudor as well as earlier styles, are often distinguishable by their low, beam-ceilings as well as by their external architectural features. In contrast with those of earlier periods, Georgian, Queen Anne, Regency and Victorian properties generally have lofty, spacious rooms.

A good deal of Dutch architectural influence may be detected in houses in what is called Queen Anne style. They are outstanding because of their steeply pitched roofs and gables. There is an air of elegance about these buildings, many of which are found in East Anglia.

While the true Georgian house is a solid, square, well-proportioned building, Regency often introduces bow windows. In general its windows are longer and narrower than their Georgian counterparts. Victorian architecture, usually Gothic in tendency, is most renowned for the sites chosen for the houses. The buildings are highly embellished in some instances and invariably there are high ceilings and bow windows, or, at least, bays of some kind.

Many of the country's biggest houses were built in the days of Victoria. Victorian tycoons had a penchant for choosing splendid sites for their homes which in many cases turned out to be rambling three-storey piles which tested the ingenuity and strengths of the domestic staffs looking after the family's needs. At the same time, the smaller Victorian houses are generally in fashion as soundly-built properties well suited for children as there is plenty room for them to cavort and enough bedroom space to accommodate them all comfortably. Other types of property are apt to attract their own values and do not easily fall into general categories. This goes for cottages, the 'twee' styles, which may be anything from a small one-room-up-and-one-room-down specimen to a full-blooded five- or six-bedroom example which is a cottage in name only. There are in addition Georgian homes which are always popular. These too, range between small terrace houses to huge country mansions, as do many of the Tudor and Elizabethan properties which have been preserved.

In some cases it is possible to find a home in one of these substantial properties as owners have had them divided up to form separate dwellings, either as flats or as complete houses. An advantage is that occupants can usually enjoy a large garden and, in addition, a reasonable amount of privacy as such large houses were invariably built in the centre of equally large estates. The choice is there, only limited by the capacity to pay!

As any owner will testify, the drawback with most period properties is that the fabric requires almost constant attention in order to keep it up to scratch. Repairs and maintenance costs increasingly make the task of preserving our older buildings more prohibitive. In addition, period buildings are 'listed' by local authorities which give them a particular status from an architectural and historical point of view. Listing means, apart from the interest generated in them, that there must not be any alteration without the consent of the local authority concerned, and repairs must conform to the original structure in style and materials used. It can be immediately deduced, as a result, that while ownership of a period house is a feather in anyone's cap, it is an adornment which must be paid for in ever-rising costs. Most owners will agree that their hands are never out of their pockets for funds to execute even the minimum work considered necessary to maintain their properties in weatherproof condition.

Pest control It can be a very wise precaution to call in some expert organization like Rentokil where older properties, and indeed where some of the not-so-old homes are concerned as well, to ensure that the place has a clean bill of health. Such firms undertake surveys, which are normally free, with a guarantee of 20 years for any work subsequently carried out.

Services by these firms range between installation of damp-proof courses to ridding homes of pests, and costs depend upon how much and how extensive the operation decided upon is.

Modern methods of damp-proofing have simplified things. Today, electro-osmotic systems requiring only a mortar joint or two to be chased out and copper strip electrodes inserted are used extensively. Alternative processes are adopted according to the types of walls involved. For damp-proofing all walls in a detached four-bedroom house or cottage the cost would be £300 to £400, possibly a bit less or a bit more depending upon the extent of the job.

Unlike dry rot, wet rot does not spread. The latter is controlled simply by replacing affected timbers, invariably window frames. To treat roof timbers for dry rot, wet rot and woodworm would cost around £200 for a straightforward job in an average-size cottage. Bigger places with complications would obviously cost more and there are instances where replacement timbers are necessary and timber is in itself an expensive item. If it is decided too, that roof insulation would be improved by a layer of special material a square metre costs about £1. This gives a three-inch deep layer of insulation.

Planning regulations Home improvements which involve extensions of more than a fifth of the existing area of a house (or industrial premises) require consent under planning regulations. Such consents are given by the planning authority for the area in which the building concerned is situated.

To obtain planning consent the appropriate form, obtained from the local council office, must be completed. The form requires full details of the work to be carried out along with plans and measurements, normally drawn as working drawings, from which a contractor would be able to estimate the amounts and costs of materials.

Sometimes extensions may interfere with a neighbour's enjoyment of his present amenities and he has the right to object. Councils acquaint neighbours with proposals for extensions. Consent too of the mortgagee is necessary if the property is being bought with the help of a mortgage. A leaseholder will require the acquiescence of the ground landlord. In all cases, work done has to comply with building by-laws and regulations so that it is advisable to seek guidance from the local authority anyway.

Plumbing Special attention should always be paid to keeping the plumbing system operating efficiently. The water supply should function properly at all times and the slightest fault should be attended to without delay. House-owners should acquaint themselves with all taps, the main one especially so that in an emergency the water may be turned off completely. In any event it is a sound idea to turn off the main tap when leaving a house for any lengthy period, say a weekend or when going on holiday. Parts of the system may be shut off separately; the feeds to and from the central heating system and to the hot water tank and cylinder. The householder should know where the various taps are located so that he can reach them with a minimum of delay. It is a wise precaution to turn taps off and on a few times so that they do not get rusted up or otherwise too tight to move. Lagging should be used to protect pipes from frost and in this respect any outside feeds, say to a w.c. are particularly vulnerable. Plumbing is for plumbers so apart from minor jobs it is better to call in the skilled man for attention to any major defect.

Porches Built either on to the back or front, porches are very useful conservers of heat. A great deal of heat loss during winter months is due to opening and closing of doors; a porch with a door which may be kept shut while an inner one is opened, helps to prevent heat loss. Many who have had porches built also find them useful little adjuncts to the windowsill for bringing on seedlings and, later, for maintaining a show of flowers.

Possessory title Where there is some doubt about the ownership of a property the Land Registry may so describe the person in possession. It means that the Registry is not satisfied with the ownership but only that the person named is in possession of the property. Where there is no such defect there would be title absolute or good leasehold title.

Private treaty A contract for the sale of a property agreed to between the parties as distinct from a sale by auction.

Property for business Various possibilities provide opportunities for home owners to do 'a little something on the side'. Most obvious is to let off rooms where a house is too large, or to maintain part of a building in flats from which an income may be received. There are several buyers who take on larger-than-necessary properties because they can obtain them more cheaply so that they can take in lodgers or convert them to flats and so help out with mortgage repayments. In these circumstances the consent of the mortgagee is necessary.

Other methods include taking over a pub, a country house which could be made into an hotel, a smallholding, or a farm. The pub and country house-cum-hotel provide a family with living quarters while producing an income too. Pubs are often not available for outright purchase but are 'tied houses' so that managers are required to run them for their brewery owners. Running a pub or hotel of course, is not everyone's glass of beer and a certain amount of training or experience is helpful to both manager/owner and customer. Both are hard work but can be rewarding.

A former large house in the country which is operating as an hotel or club does provide the chance for a more rurally-orientated family to gain both an income and a pleasant life well removed from town dwelling. One can expect to pay more for an established hotel or club, naturally, though these sometimes are offered at much less than anticipated. It all depends upon the circumstances; if they have been operating under a management system and are being sold off by the owners, a family may very well be able to come to an acceptable deal which will give them a country home and a business to pay for it. Where a country house is acquired for starting an hotel or club, planning consent for a change of use is necessary and other regulations such as fire precautions are to be considered. These can be costly; loans to start such ventures are not easily obtained. It might be more practicable to take on a lesser place and merely open a tearoom. Many families who have embarked on that course have been extremely successful.

As a nation of shopkeepers, many of us hanker for a shop with living accommodation above. Generally, the living accommodation in this type of premises is incidental to the retailing use, so the price of such property is more likely to be geared to the potential turnover of the shop than to the flat above. A number of specialist firms of business agents act as estate agents for shops as well as restaurants and licensed premises. In smaller towns the house agent may well also deal in this type of property.

One important point to remember when buying such a shop is that unless there is separate access to the upstairs home it is virtually impossible to let out the shop, so, if you tire of keeping shop, you will be forced to sell your home as well.

Smallholdings and farms have a general appeal to the British, who it would appear, are all agriculturists at heart! Smallholders, as distinct from farmers, may find it difficult to acquire land exactly where they would like it, though smallholdings do exist in varying numbers and sizes in the West Country, the Midlands, in Scotland and Wales.

There is no stipulated size for a smallholding. Where the land is heavy-cropping, such as in the Vale of Evesham and in Kent, the

Garden of England, orchards and horticultural pursuits tend to make purchasing an expensive business. In more remote areas where the land is sufficient to keep pigs or poultry, smallholdings may be much less expensive.

In parts of the country, it is generally accepted that smallholdings are from two to say 15 or 20 acres. In others, a smallholding might go to as high as 50 acres. Much depends upon whether the holding can be worked by a man and his family without outside labour or whether indeed, it can be almost a hobby, with the owner having another job and tending the land in his spare time.

Prices depend very much upon the type, size, age and state of the house. Some smallholdings have quite modern bungalows and obviously, buyers are paying for the living quarters rather than the land; other smallholdings have poorly-built and poorly-equipped houses but productive acres so that the wealth is really bound up in the land and the house is almost 'thrown in'.

No one seems to be ready to commit himself to the point at which a smallholding ends and a farm begins. There appears to be a debate between 50 and 100 acres though at the latter acreage a property would fairly be described as a farm, a farmery or perhaps a residential-agricultural estate.

Normally to qualify as a farm it will require a range of farm buildings as well as a house. Farmers now put much more store (or at least their wives and families do) on the quality and convenience of the farmhouse itself, so that, in addition to the value of the land, the value of the farmhouse must be taken into account. Farms are generally assessed as being worth so much an acre, which embraces farmhouse, buildings and land but it is clear that those having exceptional houses lift the value per acre much higher than where there is an indifferent house even if the farm buildings and land are top rate.

The country's largest farms may have two or three farmhouses on them as well as a host of cottages and farm buildings. These can be relics of the past which have been absorbed into a single unit by amalgamations over the years. It is thus sometimes possible to get a former farmhouse with maybe a couple of acres, as a country home and there could be a small range of farm buildings along with it which could it necessary be converted to provide further integral or separate accommodation. Farmhouses which are easily hived-off are usually only dispensed with in that fashion. Others, if they are in the centre of a unit are invariably part of the accommodation which a farmer provides for his senior staff.

Difficult to define too, are the residential-agricultural estates, which really may be any size from 20 to 2,000 acres. The principal attraction of such properties is the main house which might easily have as its immediate grounds, landscaped gardens and several acres of parklands. Often what are described as farmeries are operated in conjunction with a medium-size residential-agricultural property and several are found in the Home Counties where farms tend to be much smaller than in Yorkshire and Northumberland, Cumberland and Scotland or the hill holdings of Wales. The latter may be acquired in small packets too, though some of those are remote and therefore relatively inexpensive as they can be also in Cumbria.

Property insurance It should be stressed that immediately a binding contract for the purchase of a house or flat is completed the buyer becomes responsible for its insurance and if there is a loan on the property the lender will generally ensure that it is insured for fire risks. Separate arrangements are necessary to cover other eventualities.

Property register A section of the register of the properties having registered titles at the Land Registry. It provides the exact description of a property.

Proprietorship register Another section of the properties having registered titles at the Land Registry. It sets out the name and address of a registered proprietor who is the current owner and shows the price paid for his property.

Q

Queen Anne Many town and country houses built in the days of Queen Anne between 1702 and 1714 have features which are now associated with that period. Some are difficult to distinguish from those of the William and Mary styles which preceded them. Queen Anne buildings border on the Georgian. A good deal of Dutch architectural influence is evident. Much brick and stone was used in construction. Many are three-storey, with steeply pitched roofs and they have an air of elegance.

Quoins Corner stones in buildings at the angle of the walls. They are used to provide architectural variety by being placed at intervals between other stones or bricks.

R

Rack rent A rent representing the full yearly letting value of a property. The opposite is a ground rent which is payable in smaller sums since a large capital figure has been sunk in the acquisition of a lease.

Rateable value Every property is given a rateable value on which the yearly rates payable are assessed. The rateable value is calculated by the Inland Revenue taking into account various considerations which include repairs, insurance and other expenses which are incurred in maintaining a property in good condition. Attention is also paid to the values of other properties in the area. When expenses are deducted, the rateable value of a property is arrived at. New homes are given a rateable value after being inspected by the Inland Revenue's valuation officer though meantime they may be given an estimated figure.

Rate rebate Some ratepayers whose incomes fall below a certain level after taking into account allowances for dependants, qualify for a rebate on their rates. Tenants and owner-occupiers are eligible for rate rebates if their rates are not paid through a social security supplementary grant. As actual rate payments are related to income, applications should be made to the local authority finance department which issues a form to be completed for consideration.

Rates The yearly levy on occupants to pay for services provided by central and local government. Amounts payable are worked out on the value of a property which in practice is loosely the rent at which that property would be let in a free and unfettered market. Rates go towards payment for education, local authority housing, police, highways and transport, social services, sewerage and drainage services, refuse collection and disposal, parks, baths, fire services, town planning, libraries and so on. Authorities are eligible for Government grants to help out, including one for council housing developments. In addition a water rate is levied by the appropriate water authority, based on a percentage of the valuation of the property.

Much debating goes on about the fairness or otherwise of the existing rating system and the Conservative Party is in general terms ready to scrap it and replace it with some other form of local taxation or levy. During 1976 a committee headed by Sir Frank Layfield, QC, considered alternatives and one of the recommendations made to the Secretary of the Environment was that future rates should be based on the value of a house, instead of the long-established system of using rentability.

The shortage of rented property which has progressively been seen has detracted from the practicability of using rents as bases for rates simply because the theory is that the rents involved must be those obtained in a realistically free market where there is choice.

If the value system were adopted, estimates given were that owners of cheaper houses would have their rates cut considerably while those owning higher-value homes would be faced with higher bills.

It was considered that a revision of the rating valuations would take six years. Valuation officers will inspect areas choosing typical properties on which to base their new assessments. These, it was suggested would be introduced over several years. Rateable values and the actual amounts of rates to be paid would of course continue to vary from place to place, depending upon the rate in the £ levied by the relevant local authority. Obviously, where houses are most expensive, say around London and the South-East, owners could be paying higher amounts than for equivalent houses in other parts of the country but the actual figures would depend on how much revenue the local council was required to raise. If some London assessments were high but the rate in the £ levied were relatively low there could be little difference in actual payments compared with another area where assessments were low but the rate in the £ levied very high. In all cases however, those in the highest-value homes would be paying more than under the present system and those in least expensive houses less.

Real property or **real estate** Terms used in law for freehold land and houses, to distinguish it from personal property which covers all other forms. Before 1925 real property and personal property in the event of death descended in different ways. The two kinds are still valued separately as there are legal differences between them.

Redeeming a mortgage It is possible to redeem a mortgage, that is pay off a loan, before the term for which it was initially issued has expired. To redeem a mortgage the mortgagor is also obliged to meet any outstanding interest and the expenses for redemption. More financial institutions however are waiving the costs of redeeming mortgages. Several building societies have dropped their previous arrangements whereby the mortgagor was faced with charges when paying off a loan early. It was customary for borrowers who paid up their loans inside the first five years to be faced with payments amounting to three months' interest on their mortgages. Many societies still make an early redemption charge should a loan be repaid at any time before the expiration of the term for which it was initially granted.

In a number of other cases societies institute a payment depending upon the outstanding balance of the loan at the time the borrower pays. It is not usual for a society to make a charge for redemption of a loan in those instances when a new and larger mortgage is being taken out with the same society. Few people these days pay off their mortgages early as it is to their benefit from a tax angle to maintain them, albeit to a lesser degree as the period for which the loan was granted nears its end.

Societies introduced the redemption charges because of the high administration costs associated with granting a loan, particularly in its early years. At that time societies also were concerned not to make it too easy for mortgagors to move from house to house. House prices too, were markedly lower in those days than they are now so that mortgages were very much smaller.

Register The record of properties registered at the Land Registry. It has three sections; the property, the proprietorship and the charges register.

Registered proprietor The owner of a property having had its title registered at the Land Registry and shown in the proprietorship section.

Registered title Eventually it is planned, all freehold and leasehold properties will have registered titles, that is details of ownership registered at the Land Registry. Such registration is a guarantee that the person named on the title deed is the owner.

Restoration Increasingly the change in attitudes towards old buildings as well as the rising costs for new homes, is prompting more people to consider rehabilitation. Some local authorities are physically cooperating and encouraging owners by creating new cul-de-sacs of restored houses with flower beds and open areas maintained by the council. At the same time there must be careful consideration so that costs for renovation and improvements do not exceed the value of the property, a situation which has arisen in the case of country cottages in a number of areas. Price levels are sensitive and just because an expensive facelift has been given will not guarantee that it will fetch an enhanced price for the basic property itself.

Price is the hub on which all else turns and a buyer must expect to pay for what he gets . . . least for the near-derelict shell and most for the lavishly-equipped and well-maintained property which is a cottage in name only.

In the end they may work out to be not very much different in value. The shell, usually requiring the full treatment and possibly already having had a demolition order served on it in its existing state, will require complete rebuilding. Local authorities are invariably sympathetic to applications seeking to revoke demolition orders where it is proposed to renovate them to habitable standards.

On the question of grants for improving older properties there is a Department of the Environment booklet called 'Your Guide to House Renovation Grants', which may be picked up direct from the department's various offices in the regions or can be seen at any local library or citizens' advice bureau.

Another handbook on rehabilitation has been published by the *Architects Journal*. In it are aspects of repair and maintenance of older buildings with suggestions about their improvement and conversion. Particularly topical is the fact that buildings must not only be brought up to acceptable modern standards, but that they must also be re-designed in many cases to accommodate smaller family groups and single people. All these subjects are touched on with practical information about how to deal with them.

The council in whose area a shell stands, if that is the correct term for some of the tumbledown structures bought by people, will indicate such standards as will be expected, as well as indicating whether or not a grant will be forthcoming to assist with basic installations and also, whether or not there could be a further discretionary grant for general improvements.

Under the discretionary grants system a council is empowered to contribute up to half the additional amounts spent on what are considered to be necessary improvements. Grants however are not handed out without full investigation and interrogation. Anyone seeking grants should first talk over his plans with the home improvement official at the local council offices.

Always remember that without the necessary consents a council can insist that any building work done should be dismantled. By following the rules and being guided by council officials who are only too willing to give the benefit of their experience, life can be a great deal less harrowing, and, much more to the point, the job can be a great deal less worrying.

The maximum rate of grant for all home improvements is now 75 per cent for priority cases, 65 per cent in general improvement areas and 50 per cent elsewhere. For hardship applicants, these percentages can be increased. Major changes to the home improvement grant system were introduced from December 15, 1980, under which eligible expense limits for all grants were increased (see below):

	In Greater London £	Elsewhere £
Improvement Grants		
—priority cases	11,500	8,500
—non-priority cases	7,500	5,500
Repair Grants	5,500	4,000
Intermediate Grants		
—standard amenities:		
bath/shower	375	285
water to bath	475	360
basin	145	110
water to basin	250	190
sink	375	285
water to sink	315	240
WC	565	430
—Repairs	3,500	2,500
Special Grants		
—standard amenities	As for intermediate grants	
—means of escape from fire	9,000	6,750
—repairs	3,500	2,500

Regulated and secured tenants in the private and public sector are now able to apply for grants for the first time, as are prospective purchasers of houses. To help those on low incomes, mandatory intermediate grants will also be available for the first time for putting in single standard amenities, such as an inside toilet, and local authorities have wider discretion to waive the standards for other kinds of grant-aided work.

Again, what a council contributes depending upon the situation of the property is variable. A cottage or house in a housing action area can rank for a grant of 75 per cent, or, in cases of hardship up to 90 per cent of the eligible expense. In general improvement areas it is 65 per cent and elsewhere 50 per cent.

Among items which are covered by grants are bathrooms, hot and cold water supplies, inside w.c.s and kitchen sinks, with, where applicable, defects in structures such as the absence of damp-proof courses, rectification of inadequate staircases, poor lighting, ventilation and storage.

On occasions, councils are prepared to make loans to cover an owner's share of the costs involved. In certain circumstances it may be possible to arrange for payment of interest only on these loans while postponing the repayments on capital. Obviously grants and loans by councils are subject to the overall availability of funds and to government policy on lending which can change from time to time, again based on how solvent, or otherwise, the country is at any given point.

If an owner is in breach of conditions laid down by a council; say there are grants paid and a cottage is used as a second home; then a local authority is empowered to demand repayment in whole or in part, including interest, of the moneys involved. Since the sale of such a property would also involve a breach of the regulations the seller would generally be required to repay any grant voluntarily.

In addition to the installation of basic necessities, a question of putting a cottage or house into its most comfortable condition is very much up to an individual. Standards of comfort and degrees of necessity vary and the prudent purchaser of a cottage normally requires the professional services of an architect or surveyor to obtain the best deal for his outlay.

One or the other, or possibly both, can smooth the way through the statutory procedures and as well as making available their professional advice, can often recommend building firms or workmen experienced in the type of jobs which need to be done.

As a rough and ready guide, a purchaser of a cottage for modernizing should count on expending not less than he has already paid for the structure. As building costs rise, then that amount rises too, so that it is probably wise to count on an outlay of twice as much as the basic building has already cost. In almost every case the final bill is likely to be more than anticipated, not only because materials and labour have cost more but because owners invariably ask for extra bits and pieces to be included as the work continues and, imperceptibly, these tot up to considerable sums. It is very necessary therefore to keep a strict check and to have a fair idea of what these extras are going to add up to in the end.

Some funds should always be put by for the emergency too. In old buildings it is not always appreciated that snags can crop up which require treatment but which were not apparent when work started. Time and money are needed to meet such bills.

There is also a move for building societies and local councils to sponsor schemes under which local authorities buy empty substandard houses in urban situations and offer them to applicants on their lists or on their estates on condition that they are improved with the help of a grant. The local authority would organize the renovation work and a building society would provide the mortgages on the improved property valuations. According to Government circles such a scheme would increase the improvement of old property as well as encouraging more owner-occupation in lower-price categories with the direction of more building society funds involved in regenerating city areas which have been allowed to run down.

Retirement Seeking a retirement home is obviously quite a different operation from buying a first house or changing residence during a lifetime's work. Retirement presents a different set of circumstances as well as a different set of values. The first and most important question to ask is 'Do I wish to move at all from my present home?'. If the answer is 'Yes' then there are basic ways of going about things.

Doubtless, over the years, many people have built up an idea of their favourite retirement home, not excluding the 'roses-round-the-door' country cottage. For some, that prospect has receded with age and/or infirmity and a flat is the only real answer; and a ground floor one at that! Others have in their mind's eye the wonderfully blissful times spent at certain places on holiday and have always fancied that *that* is where they will retire to when the time comes. Holidays in the summer months however, do not generally reveal a town or village in its true light for the remainder of the year and coastal resorts can be gusty and inhospitable during the winter.

Many people have lived in one spot for most of their lives simply and mainly because it was there that it was most convenient for work and they may have no peculiar allegiance to it other than that. Against this they have built up friendships which they may be loath to stretch by distance.

If, after due consideration, the strain of continuing to reside in one's haunts for 40 or 50 years is too great and a move is contemplated, it should be done with great attention to detail. Some people go for the house they desire, others for the place, and so there is likely to have to be some compromise in any case. The country cottage can be a lonely cut-off prison in the winter months if it is miles from transport and shops. There is the added hazard that, for those used to city and town dwelling, entertainment will be non-existent or only provided locally by the inhabitants. Friendships are less easy to make when one is older and some communities are cagey about taking strangers into their midst until they are certain about them.

Conversely, someone who has spent a lifetime in a village may hanker after the town for his retirement. He will certainly be provided with more facilities for entertainment and communication, but could in time pine for the country pursuits and friendships which are no more easily made in cities than they are in hamlets. There is the transition possibly too, from a large to a smaller house which might be irritating for those not disposed to dispense with coveted items for which there will be only limited or indeed no, room.

Never just up sticks and go to a new area. Take time to look carefully around it; if possible have a holiday in it. Talk to the 'natives' and generally try to soak up some of the atmosphere. It may be that after sampling what was considered the top choice, a retired couple will decide to stay where they are but in a smaller house.

As far as the type of house is concerned, that is a personal choice governed as much by availability of funds as by anything else. Traditionally, retired people have plumped for the bungalow, but as the years have gone on, bungaloid estates have been pushed farther and farther from town centres. An alternative may be a flat or maisonette, maybe even an older but well-modernized terrace house. Both are likely to be closer to the shops and services than a new bungalow.

Coastal resorts can be dreary in the winter months and many retirees are now seeking places where there are interests and activities for them all the year round, which is why University cities are today among the most popular retirement centres. It is also a useless operation buying a house or bungalow with a large garden if it is obvious that it will be or become a burden in a short time.

Builders and developers have found by experience that nine out of ten buyers who are looking around for the home to serve them for the rest of their days want a bungalow and that only when one or the other partner is left on his or her own do flats come into their own, but only those at ground and first-floor levels!

Planning officials are reluctant to allow bungalow developments mainly because they use up greater areas of land, so some builders have produced courtyard styles. In these, bungalows are constructed around a communal area, some in terraces, others linked or in some way sited so as to take up a minimal amount of outside space. Obviously gardens for the individual suffer but then that suits some of the older inhabitants who find that pursuit too strenuous for their years.

The active retired couple like the bungalow because they can carry out day-to-day renovations themselves without resorting to ladders and scaffolding. Painting becomes an easy chore for the husband; there are no stairs to carpet or climb, for the wife; heating can be economical with minimum outlay for proper insulation and, when the time comes, the bungalow is one of the most saleable of buildings.

As is the case with other houses, the public prefers, but does not always get, nor is able to afford, bungalows on individual sites rather

157

than on estates. The newer ones, as with houses generally, have made concessions to the modern age by using less wood and more plastics, more concrete and fewer bricks and contain additional fitments in kitchens and bathrooms. Central heating combined with stricter attention to conserving it through adequate insulation, is the rule rather than the exception unless there is some 'building down' to a price rather than up to a standard.

Builders and developers do evaluate carefully, areas which are considered not only suitable but which have a proven record of attraction for the retired. South-coast towns such as Worthing, Eastbourne, Bournemouth and Brighton, Bexhill and Seaford traditionally attract the more elderly but in recent years there have been attempts, varying in their degrees of success, to widen the scope of employment to keep the younger elements in those places. Not surprisingly, the younger couples are equally amenable to bungalows and numbers of the elderly have been weaned over to flats which have gone up in some profusion along the coast generally.

Rarely contemplated by builders are schemes for bungalows which necessitate climbing hills, though in Devon towns like Torquay that can hardly be avoided. There are however, considerable numbers of developments of bungalows along the coasts of Devon and Cornwall, Dorset and Hampshire, and Somerset where Weston-super-Mare and Minehead have their quotas. On the Kent coast the Thanet towns, Margate, Ramsgate and Broadstairs have long catered for the retired and vast bungalow estates are to be seen there but these, with Folkestone, are today endeavouring to obtain a wider spread of age groups by introducing industry and commerce where possible.

Climatic conditions mean that the most hardy make for the Atlantic coast of Cornwall and the North-Sea areas of England from East Anglia to the Scottish borders. As far as Merseyside is concerned, they tend to go south-westwards into north Wales or on to the Lancashire coast at Southport, Morecambe Bay, Blackpool and Lytham St Annes. There is an increasing interest for retirement in the Yorkshire resorts of Bridlington, Filey and Scarborough where the emphasis is principally on flats which in many cases have replaced hotels.

Among the more coveted inland areas are those with an 'away-from-it-all' atmosphere, now sought not only by retired couples but by those who wish to give up the rat race. These days properties in the Lake District, the Yorkshire Dales, the Derbyshire Peak, and in Scotland, the sheltered environments of the western glens and seaboards are all keenly sought out.

Prices for bungalows, as well as for flats, vary with location. In all cases sea views put up the figure by anything from £1,000 to £10,000 depending upon the basic article; country views also raise prices but not to the same extent.

Right of light   Ancient lights, the right of a person owning a house to enjoyment of existing light which might be lessened should there be a building erected which might interfere with it.

Rights of way   Precautions should always be taken when it is proposed to buy a property that it is not subject to a right or rights of ways. A right of way gives another party sanction to cross an owner's property for some reason. These may vary from using a path to reach a house otherwise inaccessible and to have a limited area possibly to stand a car or other vehicle, to using the ground for conveying electricity cables or gas mains, water and drainage pipes and so on. In solicitors' parlance such rights are known as easements. Rights of way over a person's property may be acquired by grant or unrestricted use over a number of years. A right of way which is common to owners of adjoining properties must not be obstructed by anyone. Some rights of way are rights to water and any obstruction of a person's right to water is actionable. Where rights of way require to be repaired the costs are divided unless there is a provision for otherwise dealing with the question in the deed or lease.

Ring main circuit   The up-to-date type of electrical installation is the ring main circuit. It is based on 15 amps and power sockets are fused with 13-amp fuses for safety. Other electrical equipment should be fused according to the manufacturer's instructions, some items require only 2-amp fuses. Almost daily simpler and more efficient equipment is being introduced. Potential purchasers of existing homes should check that they do not require rewiring; usually the local Electricity Board will inspect the premises and advise on the state of the existing circuit.

Road charge   Occasionally owners of properties along a certain road will be subject to road charges for making up, repairing or otherwise maintaining the road. The charges are normally assessed in accordance with the length of frontage of each house. Where private estates have been developed and preserved road charges are commonly imposed.

S

Scotland   Because of the difference between England and Scotland insofar as house-purchase is concerned, it is essential that prospective buyers of Scottish properties should adopt a procedure which safeguards them.

Houses are advertised in the usual way, in Scotland most being handled directly by solicitors though estate agents are beginning to be more prominently involved. In making it known that a certain property is for sale, the solicitor or agent will ask for offers, probably indicating the area in which such offers should be made. Frequently no indication is given of the level at which offers might be started.

Once a buyer has found a house he wishes to acquire, a building society should be asked to make a survey. On receipt of a satisfactory report from the society, then it is prudent to go ahead either through a solicitor or personally and make an offer for it.

Letters, which are known as missives, play a major part. A buyer making an offer will have it accepted or rejected by the seller via one or more missives. An offer to purchase becomes binding on the person making it when the seller accepts it and a contract is automatically assumed. An offer however, is said to be accepted only when it is unconditional.

If the seller makes additional conditions, or the purchaser indicates that his offer is subject to certain conditions, nothing is binding until both parties agree. It is obviously essential that all the facts about a property are known before an offer is made otherwise acceptance could cause irremediable problems.

A surveyor's report may seem like an unnecessary expense, but it is a precaution well worth taking. For a £15,000 house a valuation fee of something around £30 is considered normal though a valuer would add a mileage charge where he expected to travel some distance from his office to do an inspection. For a full survey something approaching £100 would be more likely. These fees of course, may be varied and a full structural survey by an expert in the field could well cost much more, though in the case of a property in which there were genuine fears that there may be something wrong or that considerable outlay would be required to put it into the necessary habitable condition the money is well spent.

All through, remember the onus is on the purchaser to watch his step. The motto is 'buyer beware' and it is as well to heed it.

As in England some houses are sold by auctions, called roups in Scotland. The procedure is similar to that in England but it is more usual for Scottish auctioneers to disclose a reserve price before the sale, generally when the announcement of an auction is given.

Search The legal name for finding out information about what might happen to a property if a buyer goes ahead with acquiring it. A search is undertaken to establish whether or not there are encumbrances such as road widening proposals or the threat of compulsory purchase and so on. The search or searches are made among records kept by an official body, the local authority, Land Registry or Land Charges Registry.

Search certificate The document issued as a result of a search.

Second homes These are generally holiday or weekend retreats. Finding finance for second homes can be a problem. A fact to be faced is that mortgages are not normally available for them through channels other than private. That means borrowings for such a purpose are expensive and at interest rates above what the moneys involved could be invested for elsewhere.

Though building societies generally do not include questions on application forms about whether or not a property is for a second home, a specific inquiry would elucidate that societies are disinclined to advance funds for that purpose.

The tax man will not allow relief on mortgages for second homes and in any case there is no tax relief on any mortgage above £25,000. When a property comes to be sold, an owner of a second home will be required to state which is his principal residence. He is then due for capital gains tax on the other. He is only allowed to claim exemption from tax on his principal residence, usually the property he has lived in longest.

All details of properties owned must be given to the inspector of taxes though there is nothing in taxation law to say a man cannot have a loan on a second home.

Schemes are available for purchasing second homes abroad by using the enhanced value of a house in this country to finance a purchase elswhere. Many home-owners who bought years ago have been sitting on increasing assets and that factor can be made to work by using the money content in the present-day value of a house to help in the acquisition of an apartment or villa overseas.

An attraction of this method was that until 1974 such an arrangement qualified for tax relief, now it is not so. The amount of the loan advanced was limited only by the ability of the borrower to repay it.

In the case of Owners' Services Ltd., a development and holiday firm operating on the Continent, a scheme of that nature was embarked upon with Scottish Life Assurance Co. Through Scottish Life a first mortgage, a second mortgage, a re-mortgage or secured bank loan would be arranged. An obvious stipulation was that the security for such borrowings had to be other than on the overseas property being bought. All legal costs as well as the currency investment premium to be met would be covered by the loan.

A repayment term varying between two and 25 years was offered to prospective purchasers; in all cases life assurance cover was an integral part of the scheme.

Security   Various measures can be taken to make it more difficult for a thief to break into your home.

What has to be guarded against is the casual thief, the youngster who attempts stealing as a result of carelessness by home-owners, possibly drunks who roll into an open door or window or the 'trades-man' who is supposed to be doing one job but is really out to do another!

A professional thief on the other hand is a skilled operator who is adept at picking locks, removing glass from windows and doors by

161

stealth and working quickly and silently when entry has been gained, sorting out the real from the imitation. However, even he is likely to go next door if he finds your house is well-protected. The first step is always to ensure that it looks as if someone is at home. Varying comings and goings is a valuable tactic as is the opening and closing of different windows, doors and gates at different times.

The crime prevention officer at the local police station is always ready to give advice and assistance and will visit a house to indicate in a practical way what can and should be done.

Good locks are essential and a deadlock rather than a cylinder lock should be fitted. The best and more offputting for the potential burglar are those which are sunk into the door so that any break-in, even were it successful, would involve effort as well as noise as the bolt has to be cut or the wood smashed.

Locks and bolts can be fitted to windows too; if the windows are metal, there are special types for the purpose and locksmiths who instal door furniture will also do these jobs. Under £50 will generally take care of all the necessary alternative locks on both doors and windows.

Windows accessible from drainpipes at first- or second-floor level are a weak point. Drainpipes can be painted with special non-drying paint. There are plastic films which can be stuck on to the inside of a pane so that even if glass is broken the fragments are held in place, not foolproof of course but a nuisance to a thief who thought all he had to do was break a window and enter. The same applies to double glazing. Some people fit burglar alarms wired to the local police station and these are considered a deterrent to all but the most ingenious.

Even when people are in a house they should take care over unlocked doors. Television has provided the thief with a new source of cover for his activities. Several homes have been burgled while the family were sitting in one room enthralled by celluloid thieves while real ones were at work to their detriment in the next!

Life is getting more perplexing, however, for the housebreaker. Electronics are making it more difficult for him to follow his intentions. Prudently-set 'boxes of tricks' can screech out alarms as an intruder crosses a beam or radar wave. One of the many firms of alarm suppliers will fit an appropriate system and the National Supervisory Council for Intruder Alarms carries a list of recommended firms.

Selling   Selling a house is just as complicated as buying one, perhaps more so. Below is a suggested sequence of events which should help to smooth a seller's path.

1 decide on method(s) to be used in disposing of the property (estate agent, advertising, privately). 2 fixing an asking price (valuation by surveyor if desired). 3 instruct estate agent, agreeing in writing, his commission (subject to VAT). 4 instruct a solicitor (unless do-it-yourself is proposed). 5 wait. 6 allow potential purchasers to inspect (no

need to answer questions unless willing). 7 wait until agent submits offers received. 8 accept one which appeals. 9 provide solicitor's name so that buyer can communicate with him. 10 inform solicitor about time scales (when it is proposed to move, particularly if the purchase of another home is contemplated; ideally attempts should be made to complete the sale of one home and the purchase of the other together). 11 solicitor meantime will have been preparing necessary documents (a do-it-yourselfer will need to obtain the relevant papers from whoever acted for him in the first place if he has not got them in his possession already). 12 check the documents, if there is a mortgage there will be a charge certificate instead of the deeds or land certificate. Remember, some documents may be lodged either with a solicitor, at a bank or in some 'safe' spot which usually takes some time to recall. Expect the solicitor to be in touch from time to time on these matters as he requires other details, particularly if the property is leasehold. 13 preparation of draft contract to be signed by seller and buyer and exchanged after approval. (It should be noted that the do-it-yourselfer cannot normally buy the National Conditions of Sale nor the Law Society's Conditions of Sale though he can refer to them; he can prepare his own conditions nevertheless. The documents referred to are copyrights and are purchased only by a solicitor). 14 the contract will usually specify that 10 per cent of the price of the property should be paid as a deposit. The deposit is usually held by estate agents as stakeholders until the sale is completed. 15 the seller, if he is to buy another house, may well find he needs some temporary financial help while the buyer completes his purchase. A bank will normally oblige with what is called a 'bridging loan' once the seller has a signed contract for the sale of his property. 16 on exchange of contracts the mortgagee, if any, will be informed that a date has been decided when the mortgage will be repaid (there may be up to three months' interest to pay unless the seller is taking out another loan from the same source); there will also be the seller's share of rates, water rates and if applicable, ground rent to be decided with the buyer. 17 after exchange of contracts it is safe to cancel the insurance on the house; the responsibility for that becomes the buyer's though most sellers, to be on the safe side, maintain it until after completion. 18 before moving out contact the various service people to have things like gas, electric, phone and so on attended to and meters read. Don't forget the estate agent's bills and solicitor's fees are to be met (plus VAT).

Septic tank Country areas sometimes are not connected with main drainage services so that properties built there have what is called septic-tank disposal. The septic tank works bacteriologically, breaking down solids and allowing liquids to pass into the ground naturally. Great care must be exercised by households having septic tanks as modern detergents tend to destroy bacteria if used in heavy concentrations and so defeat the whole object of the septic tank. With septic-tank disposal, wastes are fed into the tank instead of into the main drainage system.

Shared drives and paths In instances where these exist the title deeds to the properties concerned will indicate who owns drives or paths as well as those having the right to use them. Deeds may stress that one party owns the drive or path and that the other has the right of way over it, or they may show that both parties have equal ownership having half each. Neither party is entitled to obstruct a shared drive or path in any way.

Softwood Larch, spruce, pine and fir fall into this category of timber. The softwoods are of more open texture and are lighter in weight than the hardwoods.

Solicitor Professional man who undertakes the legal side of home buying. Potential purchasers of properties usually are recommended by someone, possibly an estate agent, if they do not have a family solicitor. An alternative is to look in the Law List at the local public library. The List contains the names of all solicitors (and barristers) along with the names and addresses of firms operating in the various towns and cities. Citizens' Advice Bureaux and local housing departments also carry the names of local solicitors who are ready to carry out conveyancing work in house purchase as well as to give legal advice on other matters falling within the scope of the departments, such as the legal position of tenants, disputes over ownerships and so on.

Anyone may approach a solicitor and request him to act. Remember too, he is *your* servant; you are *not* his. Your commissioning him to undertake work for you will necessitate your paying a fee. Agree with him what this will be before committing yourself or him in any way and get his terms in writing. He might not like to do this, but insist! Obviously there will be some degree of movement as far as fees are concerned because sometimes snags crop up which take longer and more unravelling than anticipated. Nevertheless, an *estimate* is of great value when the vital task of arranging finances is involved. For some time now solicitors have been unable to charge scale fees as laid down earlier by their professional body, the Law Society, for house-purchase work so there is a place for a measure of bargaining. If you don't like one you can always go to another!

Sporting rights Properties with a stretch of river or stream, perhaps some extensive land, often have sporting rights attached to them. Fishing and shooting rights are frequently mentioned separately with properties as they are either 'in hand' which means they are available to the purchaser or 'let', which indicates that they are not available until the period for which they are let expires. Sporting rights which are sold along with a property, either as being vacant and available to a buyer or as an income from them while they are let add considerably to its value.

The avid golfer likes his garden gate to open on the fairway of his favourite course, and that puts pounds on the price! Similarly enhanced are properties which face on to golf courses, a point which developers have long since noted. Parks, too, have an effect on prices though the sports followed in them can be a nuisance on occasion. Truth to tell, owners prefer houses which are not 'shut in' by other buildings and so long as there is breathing space the prices achieved will always recognize that fact.

River and sea moorings are other amenities which add to the value of properties, and a stream at the bottom of the garden for private boating is a sure winner.

Some of the sporting attributes attached to houses can be turned to income. Hunting boxes now no longer used as such have stabling which may be rented out; amenity land around them can also be grazed. Fishing rights these days may be let – syndicates are always on the lookout for suitable waters, and shooting is also greatly prized.

Stakeholder A person who holds a deposit as a third party between seller and buyer. If such a person is an estate agent and a deposit is laid with him, a receipt should always be obtained stating that he holds the money as stakeholder. A deposit then may only be passed on to a seller with the consent of the purchaser or, as the case might be, be returned to the buyer with the approval of the seller.

Stamp duty A levy paid to the Government in the case of a number of documents of agreement. The duty is payable on deeds of transfer, conveyance or assignment of property at prices above £20,000. Unless they are properly stamped the Land Registry will not accept relevant documents and title deeds, for registration of ownership.

Storage space Family clobber always has to be stowed away somewhere and there are ways of utilizing odd corners of a house which should be explored for the purpose. Apart from the kitchen, which must provide storage for the day-to-day needs of the household with a range of cupboards and shelves everywhere that there is space for them, those alcoves in dining room and drawing room can be pressed into use. Shelving can be used to advantage as can cupboards fitted below it; they make a convenient and pleasant cabinet and shelving for, say china or ornaments.

Bay windows lend themselves to a range of seating with lids so that books, papers, records can be kept underneath, while upstairs, bedrooms obviously are sitting targets for the handyman with ambitions for built-in wardrobes and dressing tables. Those less expert can find a variety of ready-to-fit units designed to slot into most spaces and there are in addition, craftsmen willing and able to do a professional job on areas which are less conventional and require more-than-ordinary treatment.

These could embrace that under-the-stairs cubbyhole which normally does little else but collect rubbish or perhaps the effective use of space above a stairwell which some people find can accommodate additional cupboards with access from the landing.

The loft is invaluable as a storage place, though only too often it contains an accumulation of junk which would be better thrown on a rubbish dump. If floored in and fitted with some shelving and storage units, the loft can be used for storing household equipment which is needed only from time-to-time. A foldaway ladder is a worthwhile investment for easy access.

Subject to contract   One of the most essential phrases used in transactions involving property transfers. It means that parties have reached a provisional agreement but have not entered into a legally binding contract. All correspondence regarding house purchase should be marked 'subject to contract' until contracts are signed and exchanged. If terms are agreed 'subject to contract' either side may withdraw from the transaction without giving any reason.

Subsidence   Can be caused by deep mine workings, erosion of cliffs or other high ground by sea or river, and the drying out of clay subsoils where foundations are faulty. Where coalmining is concerned, the National Coal Board have a compensation scheme for those whose homes are proved to have been affected by mining. Many homes built on clay were badly affected by subsidence during the long, hot, dry summer of 1976. Often underpinning or shoring up are methods employed to overcome the worst effects of subsidence.

T

Tax relief   Tax relief is given to home-buyers on the interest paid on mortgages. The amount of relief varies with the tax liability of the individual. Relief is also given on assurance policy amounts which are parallel with or additional to any mortgage figure. Thus, depending upon a person's liability for tax can be assessed which type of mortgage or mortgage/assurance is best suited to any individual. Those paying tax at the highest rates obviously find that they can obtain maximum relief. Inland Revenue rules have been relaxed so that home-owners who leave their properties for up to four years in some cases can still qualify for tax relief on mortgage interest. For years tax relief was allowed on mortgage interest only insofar as it related to the only or main residence of the borrower, his divorced or separated spouse, or a dependent relative. In determining the benefit of tax relief temporary absence of only up to a year had previously been the yardstick. Recent legislation has been amended so that a person required to move because his work in Britain or overseas necessitates it, can be eligible for tax relief for a term not expected to exceed four years, providing it can be reasonably expected also that the property will again become the mortgagor's main or only residence on his return.

There is no provision for the relief to continue beyond four years. However, if there is a further temporary absence after a person has reoccupied his home, the four-year term for relief will reapply to the new circumstances. The fact that relief was given for a previous four-year period will not influence the new situation.

Telephone and postal service   Both sellers and purchasers of a house should notify the GPO of the change. A buyer may wish to make arrangements for a telephone to be taken over and put in his name; charges up to that point are the responsibility of the seller but he will not wish to be burdened with bills for calls made after he has left the premises! Agreement to take over a phone or to remove it must be made through the GPO. Forms are available for mail to be redirected in the case of the seller and forwarded to the new address in the case of the buyer.

Title   It is incumbent upon the purchaser, either himself if he is doing it himself, or on his solicitor, to clear the title before acquiring leasehold or freehold property. The practice is known as 'investigating the title', which means that the buyer or his representative must satisfy himself that the seller has the right to sell the property he is offering; in other words that without doubt, the property is his to dispose of. The title is traceable through the deeds which show previous transactions relating to the property concerned in a deal for the previous 15 years and any point which is unclear must be clarified.

Title absolute   The Land Registry designation given to the ownership of a property when it is completely satisfied about the ownership. A house which is registered with title absolute is a state guarantee that the ownership is as stated.

Title deeds   The documents which provide evidence of ownership of a freehold or leasehold property. Generally the documents will include every deed conveying ownership over the past 15 years. Title deeds are replaced by land certificates once a property is registered at the Land Registry, (or, if the property is mortgaged, by a charge certificate).

Tools   Every householder should have a few tools for the odd jobs to be done around the property from time to time. Obviously a hammer, a pair of pliers and a screwdriver are three which spring to mind, and it is a good idea to add a few items as time goes on. Chisels and saws are useful, nails and screws of various sizes and some of the modern all-purpose tools save both energy and money. Keep them handy, in a toolbox or in a kitchen drawer. Don't forget fuse wire if the electric system is one which requires it (modern ones are more sophisticated and don't) and remember to have a card with three wire sizes for the loading each fuse has to bear. For fused plugs, the proper size fuses should also be kept in reserve.

Transfer The legal method by which the title deed to a registered property is transferred from a seller to a buyer.

Tudor Name applied to houses, usually large country homes and manors, built during the reign of the Tudor monarchs between 1485 and 1603. The building shows Gothic traces and merges with Elizabethan styles at the later date during the reign of Elizabeth I from 1558. The manors are distinctive in style and are easily recognized by the peculiar chimney stacks.

U

U-bend The fitting below lavatories, sinks and washbasins; a bend in the outlet pipe which prevents objectionable odours and is easily clogged. Modern fittings may be unscrewed easily and cleaned when this happens. It is a good idea to include an inspection of U-bends where they can be easily reached at regular intervals. Most become affected by hair or in the case of kitchens by congealed grease.

Unadopted road Roads which are below standards laid down by local authorities are termed unadopted. They may be narrower than stipulated or not finished in specified materials. Unadopted roads can be costly to the unwary house-owners and/or buyers as they will be charged for their maintenance and, possibly in due course, will be required to make a substantial payment to a council to have them brought into line with other thoroughfares prior to being taken over, that is adopted, by the council as part of its ordinary road network.

Uninvited entry The law gives an owner the right to defend and protect his property. He may take steps to restrain intruders and trespassers and to discourage them from entering his premises. At the same time he must exercise proper responsibility. That includes ensuring freedom that those people he does wish to be in his house or garden are not harmed or injured. In the ordinary way that is covered by the owner carrying out proper and regular repairs and maintenance. If his home abuts a highway used by the public he is liable for any injury resulting from debris falling from a faulty structure on to a passer-by. Insurance normally takes care of such eventualities but it is as well to check up on policies.

Keeping out the unwanted or deterring entry can be accomplished in a reasonable manner by an owner. He may implant broken glass in his boundary wall and such like but not erect electrically-charged fences which could kill. Nor must he set up dangerous traps. Even his watchdog must act within proper limits and if there is an intruder an owner is restricted to using just enough force to control or eject him. It is not considered reasonable to bear down on an unarmed intruder with a cudgel. At night an owner need not be quite so reluctant! As night-time intrusion is considered to be more frightening a bit of violence on the part of the owner could very well be overlooked by a court so long as it was deemed that he was protecting his property and any goods in it from being pinched.

In addition to invited guests and friends a host of public officials have rights of entry to houses. The owner's consent to entry is usually required but in certain circumstances, court orders are given. Bailiffs and sheriffs' officers are given wide powers of entry, local authorities can investigate for vermin and overcrowding, gas, water, electricity, post office telephone engineers and police are among those who can be given permission to enter to attend to their various duties. A Customs and Excise officer can conduct a search and even Inland Revenue men can obtain entry to assess improved or enlarged property.

Upkeep Buying a home is only the start. There are provisions in a mortgage deed or in a lease where a property is leasehold, which stipulate that a property must be maintained in good repair and adequately insured. When budgeting it is necessary to take into account the fact that there will be rates to meet, which are obligatory, bills for electricity, gas and other forms of power where applicable, all to be coped with in addition to day-to-day living costs.

Urbanization Usually a reference to a development overseas. It is more than just a housing estate and includes generally a shopping and recreational complex. Earlier postwar urbanizations were so called because in many countries they were conjured up from virgin land in areas where no previous building, apart from the odd farmhouse or two, had ever taken place on any scale. A number of the largest urbanizations are almost new towns carrying as they do, a wide range of services.

Utility room In modern concept this is a spare room which can be used for almost anything, depending upon how a family wishes to allocate the accommodation. Much depends upon where it is built in a house; often it is brought into service as a laundry, workshop or playroom. In Victorian days and later it was very much *the* utility room, housing the cleaning gear of the household along with bits and pieces for the upkeep of the house – ironing tables, buckets, brooms, mops and tools, jumbled up with gardening jackets and football boots. In older houses which have been modernized the former utility room is frequently converted into a ground-floor cloakroom. The modern equivalent to the real utility room is usually the cupboard under the stairs!

V

Valuation There are few, if any, occasions when in house purchase it is not advisable to commission an independent valuation of the property. People who are selling houses and flats frequently suggest prices for them which are too high (seldom too low) and it is necessary for a purchaser to know what the property is really worth in current market conditions for its situation, size, and condition. It is best to ask a local valuer to undertake the task as he is acquainted with local factors and has a knowledge of property prices in the area. Most estate agents are valuers or have valuers on their staffs or on call. All valuers are not estate agents; in Scotland valuers usually stick to being valuers and rarely sell homes themselves.

Value Added Tax (VAT) Services provided by surveyors, solicitors and estate agents as well as other tradesmen and craftsmen attract VAT. This is a tax on top of the payment made for the service provided, for example, on the conveyancing, transfer or assignment of a house or flat.

Valuer One who carries out valuations for many purposes, including property matters and furniture. Usually a valuer is an auctioneer, estate agent, surveyor, but may not necessarily practise other than as a valuer. In Scotland they are valuators; it is normal for them to practise valuating rather than selling homes. Scottish practice for generations has been for solicitors themselves to handle house sales though they call in valuers to assess their worth. Many valuers, members of the Rating and Valutation Association, are employed in local and national government offices. Those in practice privately are also members of that organization (FRVA or AFVA) or possibly of the Incorporated Society of Valuers and Auctioneers (FSVA or ASVA) or the Royal Institution of Chartered Surveyors (FRICS or ARICS). Some valuers in practice are not qualified as members of a professional organization or they may be members of the National Association of Estate Agents (ANEA or MNEA).

Ventilation Proper ventilation of a house or flat is vital. Watch for previous misdemeanours such as blocked up air bricks, metal grids, particularly where these relate to underfloor passage of air. Generally speaking, where central heating has been installed and previous fireplaces bricked up, it is necessary to preserve some form of ventilation for which previously the chimney served. Floorboards deprived of adequate ventilation are subject to dry and wet rot. Lofts and attics similarly deprived of proper ventilation also can become infested with rot.

Victorian   Much of the building between 1840 and 1900 has the mark of the state of industry at that time; the large house of the mill-owner and businessman and the row upon row of Coronation Street tiny homes for his employees. The earliest Victorian houses can be confused with late Georgian, indeed there is no distinction in many town houses. The largest Victorian properties can rise to five or six storeys with basement, and the 'Upstairs Downstairs' television serial amply illustrated the places of both family and servants in the manner of things. Victorian houses have lofty ceilings and large rooms or low ceilings and small rooms depending upon to which end of the social scale they belong. The Victorian businessman had one redeeming instinct; his home was invariably among the best-sited in or out of town. Because of their spaciousness many of the more compact Victorian houses are sought today for family use. The small terrace properties are also pressed into service by being modernized and having basic amenities installed. In some cases this necessitates an extension to the existing building.

W

Water supply   Most homes today draw their water from public supplies. It is important to know therefore, where the stopcock is situated for turning the water on and off at the main in case of an emergency such as a burst pipe. Some of the older houses have water branch pipes from the main which are controlled by a T-iron just inside or close to the front door. Should a burst occur during a thaw after frost prompt cutting off of the main supply is necessary to avoid serious damage. There are other occasions, such as installing a new boiler, replacing a cylinder or taps when it may be necessary to cut off the main supply.

Modern building methods ensure that pipes are insulated and carried up interior walls to prevent freezing and there are few places between the stopcock and the tanks where freezing might occur. In the roof these are lagged. Tanks in the roof space should be readily accessible through a trapdoor of sufficient dimension to allow another tank of the same capacity to pass through it. Galvanized iron tanks require renewing from time to time and these days many people put in an anode which 'melts' and has to be replaced as it counteracts various acids and chemicals in the water mainly created by the association of copper piping with the tank and water. Inspection of the tank can be facilitated by boarding over the rafters around it and from it to the trapdoor. An extension electric light is of benefit too, in the loft, doing away with the fire risks associated with candles and matches.

Overflow pipes from cisterns should be completely self-draining without bends which might hold water and freeze up during the winter months. Stopcocks on pipes drawing water from the service tank for cutting off water when small jobs, such as rewashering taps require to be done, are useful. They save turning the water off at the mains. It is not generally appreciated that a leaking tap is a legal offence, the view being taken that in the event of a blocked waste pipe a leak could cause flooding.

It is impossible to indicate exactly where a stopcock will have been placed but there are broad rules to follow when trying to locate it. If there is only one stopcock it will most certainly be outside, or may be in the garage if the house it serves is part or close to it. Should a house front directly on to a street the tap will be found near the front door, or more likely in the yard at the rear. Where the house or bungalow has a garden in front it is usually to be found near the boundary wall, close to the gate. Look for it two or three feet below the surface under a hinged cover. Modern homes and flats have stopcocks inside, close to where the mains supply enters the property. The kitchen is most likely to be the place to find it, often under the sink.

Wet rot A timber defect caused by water soaking into woodwork. Wet rot is not generally as serious as dry rot but should be treated by one of the firms which specialize in righting property defects.

Will No one dies sooner by making a will! It saves a great deal of sorting out however, when the worst comes to the worst. These days, if a person is a home-owner his estate will be large enough to justify making a will. Most husbands leave everything to their wives and vice versa and the arrangement works reasonably well. Joint ownership of the family home will cut down liability to tax as the deceased will own only a half share which will be counted as an asset along with his movable property and effects. A married man with two children whose possessions, including his home, are valued at £15,000 or more will be liable under the Capital Transfer Tax which has replaced death (estate) duty. A will can ensure that payment of tax can be postponed until the death of the survivor of husband and wife.

William and Mary Houses of distinction built between 1690 and 1702 are described as William and Mary style.

Wiring It is wise to inspect wiring in a house. Buyers should find out in detail when a property was wired as wires wear out just like anything else but apart from that, technological progress has advanced styles of fuses, switches, plugs and so on. Local electricity boards undertake inspections and give advice. Older houses and bungalows especially should be rewired if they have not been done for 25 years or more. Prospective buyers should enquire about wiring when they visit a property they are intent on purchasing.

172

Woodworm   Really the larvae of beetles which feed on wood. Presence is detected by small holes and tiny mounds of rejected wood dust. Furniture is most often attacked. Woodworm can be treated by a solution of formalin or by carbolic and paraffin or fumigation can be resorted to. Specialist firms carry out the necessary treatment.

Workshop   Among outside sheds or in the garage (or in a room in the house if there is no alternative) it is a sound idea to have a work space. Handymen like to work on their own and they may as well have somewhere suitable to undertake odd jobs around the house. Outside, a workshop can conveniently be shared with a greenhouse or with the garden shed; inside all or part of a room may be set aside. In the typical three up/two down semi-detached home the small bedroom makes an acceptable workshop where it is not required for family purposes. Good lighting, either natural or artificial is a first essential. After that, one of the modern, collapsible fold-away benches is a wise investment, being efficient and saving space when not in use.

X

Xenophobia   If you are a xenophobe, you have a fear or intense dislike of foreigners and things foreign. This is an important point in choosing a district in which to live and equally it is a sound idea to check up who your neighbours might be if you would be so upset as to be ill. A seller of a property is subject to the legislation on racial discrimination so that neither he nor his agent may place any restrictions on a property being sold to any particular nationality. A buyer, on the other hand can choose where he wishes to live.

Xylophones and other musical instruments   Larger musical instruments have a habit of taking up considerable room. It is essential therefore, that for persons interested in such items, including grand pianos, the accommodation proposed or acquired should be sufficiently large to house them! Immediately, as a result, a small modern flat is usually not a suitable place, nor is a flat these days ever satisfactorily insulated should long hours of practice be called for. Obviously, those having musical talents with instruments to match should go in for properties which lend themselves in that direction. Neighbours have a case, in law, should they be disturbed by musical instruments or indeed by any other noise or nuisance.

Y

Yale lock   Term loosely used today to describe a number of similar locks. These are tumbler locks, opened by flat keys. The original Yale lock was invented by an American locksmith named Linus Yale.

Yard   Familiar area at the rear of Coronation-street-type houses, where were once accommodated the coalshed and outside w.c. Essentially an unproductive patch, mainly flagged or concreted, as distinct from a small garden.

Your own conveyancing   While for most people, the legal formalities of buying and selling a house or flat are entrusted to a solicitor, there is in law nothing to stop anyone carrying out the necessary transactions himself. Those who feel equipped for the task, with time and skills to undertake all the intricacies involved doubtless feel it well worth the business of saving money by self-service. According to the law, which some pressure groups are adamant on changing, conveyancing may only be done for profit by a solicitor whose activities are regulated by the Law Society.

This right has been challenged by several organizations, mainly a body called the National House Owners Society, which, as a service to its members, will undertake the legal aspects of purchasing. There is also much Parliamentary debate on whether or not the present practices should continue.

For those determined to proceed on their own a useful book of guidance has been produced by the Consumers' Association, which in its foreword points out that there is widespread misunderstanding about what solicitors have to do. Most people, it says, underestimate the amount of solicitors' work and the responsibility they take, mentioning that conveyancing covers a range of activities from the intricacies of trust law to the niceties of redevelopment in city centres.

According to the Consumers' Association 'Provided that a house is secondhand, fully occupied by an owner-occupier, and the title to it is already registered, an intelligent and industrious non-lawyer should be able to buy or sell without having a solicitor'.

There are aspects of a transaction which must be cleared. If a property is being handled through an estate agent, or the seller himself, it is essential to obtain the answers to the above points – title, occupation and registration, the latter question being answered if there is any doubt by reference to the title deeds.

Should everything proceed according to plan, a do-it-yourself conveyancer may wonder what all the fuss is about. However, in the words of the Consumers' Association again – 'The matter gets more complicated where the title is not registered, since deducing and investigating an unregistered title is more complicated. It is more complicated too, where the house is newly built, particularly where it is part of a housing estate'.

There is this warning too – 'At each stage through the transaction something may turn up which will defeat you and you will then, sheepishly no doubt, have to take your file to a solicitor and get him to complete the matter for you. He will probably charge you the same as if he had carried it through from the beginning. He will probably not think highly of your efforts so far. He may say he ought to charge you for unravelling the mess you have made of the matter on your own. All the same do not delay going to a solicitor if you are in any doubt or difficulty.

Legal problems may arise in the course of a transaction. What for instance, if the seller were to die or become bankrupt after a binding contract had been made but before the transaction was completed? The do-it-yourself conveyancer must then go to a solicitor who should advise and act for him. There are a number of other situations where the layman may be forced into abandoning his efforts. For this reason it is prudent to keep in reserve sufficient money to pay the solicitor's fees'.

According to solicitor Mr Michael Joseph, however, who has written a book called *The Conveyancing Fraud*, which he has published himself, the layman can quite easily do his own legal work. Mr Joseph considers that by spending £1·30 on the book, the do-it-yourself conveyancer can save himself anything from £200 to £350 each time he moves house. He deals with the legal system insofar as it relates to both house buying and selling, giving the alternatives to present methods and looks at some relevant branches of the law, including divorce. Also laid out are examples of questions and answers, forms and lists.

Pointing out that someone buying or selling a house can go to a firm of unqualified conveyancers set up in opposition to the Law Society's monopoly, Mr Joseph indicates that unless one knows a solicitor who will do the job for half-price, it makes economic sense to use one of these bodies – the National House Owners' Society, based in Harrow, Homes Conveyancing Estate Agents or Stewart Title (UK) with offices in London. They carry out the same procedures as those in solicitors' offices for considerably reduced fees.

With these factors in mind Mr Joseph asserts that when it comes to conveyancing a reasonably intelligent amateur under his guidance, is almost bound to do a better job than the professional.

The do-it-youself conveyancer must also consider that there are certain other expenses he will have to meet. If a mortgage is involved, while his solicitor's charges are saved, those acting for the building society will have to be paid, as well as stamp duty, Land Registry fees and other items for travel and inspections. For a normal transaction, say for a good three-bedroom semi-detached or small detached home in the £12,000 to £20,000 bracket, the amount of money saved by carrying through the legal formalities oneself would be between £150 and £200, barring accidents! But they are also time-consuming.

It must also be remembered that a solicitor usually has ready access to the services required by a purchaser; insurance, valuing, mortgage availability and suitability, along with advising on the best methods of purchase to gain most tax advantage, and where a question of joint ownership arises, the best method of handling that type of occupation, with safeguards and benefits or snags.

There is a middle course. Sometimes it is possible for a seller and buyer to use the same solicitor though this is discouraged because there may be points which could embarrass. Another way is to use the solicitor acting for the building society or assurance company granting a loan, though often the mortgagees insist on an independent lawyer.

Care must be exercised when laymen are concerned that the careful line of demarcation is not breached. For example it is legal for a layman to prepare a conveyance or transfer himself but not legal for him to have it prepared by an unqualified person (a third party). Bank managers too, are sensitive about the subject and if a do-it-yourselfer is counting on some financial bridge while negotiations are going on, they are likely to insist on a solicitor acting for the parties. They look upon a solicitor as some sort of guarantee that moneys advanced will be repaid when a sale is completed. There won't be any way either of circumventing building society and assurance company rules that a solicitor must handle those parts of the deal with which they are concerned, such as investigation of the title and the preparation of any mortgage deed.

Z

Zone Modern planning methods tend to place various areas into zones. We therefore have residential zones in which industries and commercial undertakings are banned, or where they are established, will be moved out in due course. Similarly, other districts are designated as industrial zones, commercial zones, shopping zones and so on.

USEFUL ADDRESSES

A

Abbeyfield Society, 35a High Street, Potters Bar, Herts.
Association of Certified Accountants, 29 Lincoln's Inn Field, London WC2.

B

Building Centre, 26 Store Street, London WC1.
Building Research Establishment, Advisory Service, Garston, Watford, Herts.
   Laboratory, Princes Risborough, Aylesbury, Bucks.
Building Societies' Association, 14 Park Street, London W1Y 4 AL.

C

City of Westminster Assurance, Ringstead House, 6 Whitehorse Road, Croydon
   CR0 2JA.
Consumers' Association, 14 Buckingham Street, London WC2.
Corporation of Mortgage & Finance Brokers, 24 Broad Street, Wokingham,
   Berks.

D

Department of Architecture & Civic Design, Greater London Council, County
   Hall, London SE1.
Department of Health and Social Security, Overseas Group, DHSS Central
   Office, Newcastle upon Tyne NE98 1YX.

E

Elderly Invalid Fund, 10 Fleet Street, London EC4.
Equitable Life, 4 Coleman Street, London EC2R 5AP.

F

Faculty of Architects & Surveyors, 15 St Mary's Street, Chippenham, Wilts.
Federation of Master Builders, 33 John Street, London WC1.
Federation of Private Residents' Associations, 83 Cambridge Street, London
   SW1.

G

Guildhall Garden Products, Guild House, Hearsall Lane, Coventry CV5 6LF.
Guardian Housing Association, Oxenford House, 13/15 Magdalen Street, Oxford OX1 3BP.

H

Hanover Housing Association, Hanover Close, 22 Sandford Rise, Danders Hill, Charlbury, Oxford.
Hambro Provident Assurance, 7 Old Park Lane, London W1Y 3LJ.
Help the Aged, 32 Dover Street, London W1.
Home Reversions, 31 Windsor Place, Cardiff.
House Owners Co-operative Ltd, Property Conveyancing, 19 Sheepcote Road, Harrow, Middlesex.
Housing Corporation, Headquarters, Maple House, 149 Tottenham Court Road, London W1P 0BN.
Regional Offices:
> London, Waverley House, 7/12 Noel Street, London W1V 3PB.
> South East (South), Prudential House, Wellesley Road, Croydon CR0 9XY.
> South East (North), Prospect House, Wyllwotts, Potters Bar, Herts EN6 2QW.
> South West, 35 Guildhall Centre, Exeter EX4 3LE.
> Wales, 24 Cathedral Road, Cardiff CF1 9LJ.
> West Midlands, Norwich Union House, Waterloo Road, Wolverhampton WV1 4BP.
> East Midlands, Phoenix House, 16 New Walk, Leicester LE1 6TE.
> North West, Elisabeth House, 16 St Peter's Square, Manchester M12 3DF.
> North East, St. Paul's House, 23 Park Square South, Leeds LS1 2ND.
> Scotland, Forth House, 13/17 Forth Street, Edinburgh EH1 3LE.
> Scotland, Headquarters, 19 Coates Crescent, Edinburgh EH3 7AF.

I

Incorporated Association of Architects & Surveyors, Jubilee House, Billing Brook Road, Western Favell, Northampton.
Incorporated Society of Valuers & Auctioneers, 3 Cadogan Gate, London SW1X 0AS.
Institute of Chartered Accountants of England & Wales, Moorgate Place, London EC2.
Institute of Cost & Management Accountants, 63 Portland Place, London W1.

M

Mutual Households Association Limited, 41 Kingsway, London WC2.

N

National Association of Estate Agents, Walton House, 11/15 The Parade, Royal Leamington Spa, Warwicks.

National Corporation for the Care of Old People, Nuffield Lodge, Regents Park, London NW1.

National Council of Building Material Producers, 26 Store Stree, London WC1.

National Federation of Builders' & Plumbers' Merchants, 15 Soho Square, London W1V 5FB.

National Federation of Building Trades Employers, 82 New Cavendish Street, London W1.

National Federation of Housing Associations, 30 Southampton Street, London WC2.

National Federation of Plastering Contractors, 82 New Cavendish Street, London W1.

National Federation of Site Operators, 31 Park Road, Gloucester.

National House-Builders Federation, 82 New Cavendish Street, London W1.

National House-Building Council, 58 Portland Place, London W1.

National House Owners' Society, 815 Lea Bridge Road, London E17.

Noble Lowndes & Partners, Norfolk House, Wellesley Road, Croydon CR9 3EB.

P

F. Pratten & Co., Midsomer Norton, Bath BA3 4AG.

Pre-Retirement Association, 19 Undine Street, London SW17 8PP.

R

Rating & Valuation Association, 115 Ebury Street, Belgravia, London SW1.

Royal British Legion Housing Association, 35 Jackson Court, Haslemere, High Wycombe, Bucks.

Royal Institue of British Architects, 66 Portland Place, London W1N 4AD.

Royal Institution of Chartered Surveyors, 12 Great George Street, London SW1P 3AD.

S

Save & Prosper Group, 4 Great St Helens, London EC3P 3EP.

Scottish Life Assurance Co., 36 Poultry, London EC2.

Shepherd Building Group, Blue Bridge Lane, Yorks.

W

William Whittingham, Ettingshall Road, Wolverhampton.

C. S. Wiggins & Sons, 57 Hart Road, Thundersley, Essex.